## DATE DUE

# THE TRANSFORMATION OF BIGFOOT

# Smithsonian Series in Ethnographic Inquiry

*William Merrill and Ivan Karp, Series Editors*

Ethnography as fieldwork, analysis, and literary form is the distinguishing feature of modern anthropology. Guided by the assumption that anthropological theory and ethnography are inextricably linked, this series is devoted to exploring the ethnographic enterprise.

# The Transformation of Bigfoot

## MALENESS, POWER, AND BELIEF AMONG THE CHIPEWYAN

*Henry S. Sharp*

SMITHSONIAN INSTITUTION PRESS
WASHINGTON AND LONDON

Editor: Deborah Corsi
Designer: Alan Carter

Library of Congress Cataloging-in-Publication Data

Sharp, Henry S.
The transformation of Bigfoot.

Bibliography: p.
1. Chipewyan Indians—Hunting.
2. Indians of North America—Northwest
Territories—Hunting.
3. Power (Social sciences)
4. Sasquatch. I. Title.
E99.C59S54 1988   306'.08997   87-26422
ISBN 0-87474-848-8

# Contents

# On Privacy

I am firmly committed to the idea that human behavior is a natural phenomenon and as such a legitimate area of investigation and analysis. I am also committed to the idea that individuals have the right to live their lives without unsought publicity. It is sometimes difficult to reconcile these two notions. The people and events described in this account are real, so to preserve their individual privacy I have taken certain precautions. Some details that do not change the ethnographic picture may have been altered. A few incidents are so revealing of Chipewyan culture that I will transport them from work to work, again provided they do not distort the ethnographic picture. The names of all Chipewyan are false as are all place names except that of the Northwest Territories. I have drawn upon other works of mine but have not referenced them. Citation of other sources has been restricted to help conceal the location of the study area. Certain of the arguments presume that specialists are familiar with two recent publications on the relationship between meaning and experience and with the operation of gossip among the Chipewyan but knowledge of these is not necessary for the general reader.

# Acknowledgments

Above all to the *dene* (the people) themselves. For nearly three years on more than eight occasions between 1969 and 1983 they shared their lives with me. Sharing the circumstances of their lives has added immeasurable richness to my own life and has given me experiences essentially impossible in our rapidly, and depressingly, urbanizing world. I can never repay what they have given; at best I can only hope this book will help a callous and insensitive larger society recognize the richness of knowledge and experience in these lives hidden so far from its mainstream.

The National Museum of Man in Ottawa provided a contract in Urgent Ethnology that paid most of the expenses for the 1975 research. I thank it for its funding, its publication of certain aspects of these events, and the superb job it has done in making the Chipewyan and other Northern Athapaskans no longer among the least-known people in North America. Some of the costs of the 1977 research were paid by the President's Research Grant at Simon Fraser University, Burnaby, British Columbia.

Over the years this work has grown from a simple account of a single incident into the more complex form presented here. As it grew, I was able to use undergraduate and graduate students at Simon Fraser University as a sounding board. They are too many to name so I must let Phil Moore, Dara Culhane, Jody A. Sondergaard, and Bernie N. M. Kowey represent them all. At Simon Fraser University I received encouragement, advice, and stimulation from fellow faculty members. I wish to thank particularly Noel Dyck, Michael G. Kenny, Beverly Gartrell, and Arlene McLaren. Professor T. O. Beidelman of New York University provided a very useful critical reading of the manuscript for which I am grateful. I received advice and consideration on the manuscript's shorter form from Ernest S. Burch Jr.,

June Helm, James G. E. Smith, and James Van Stone. Much that is of worth in this work comes from the skilled advice and insight they gave, but any errors or faults that remain are my own responsibility.

Typing of the first drafts of the manuscript were done by the secretarial staff at Simon Fraser's Department of Sociology and Anthropology under the direction of Jean Jordan. My thanks to her and her staff for their speed, accuracy, courtesy, and interest.

I spent several years after the summer of 1984 as a scholar in residence at the Department of Anthropology at the University of Virginia. The members of that department have created a stimulating ambience of scholarship and interest in social anthropology extending far beyond their own specialties. I wish especially to thank Edie Turner, Chris Crocker, David Sapir, and Peter Metcalf for their comments.

For ten years I was married to a Chipewyan, Bernadette Sharp. I am grateful for her help and insight into her culture, but it should not be thought that my analysis expresses her own view. The two of us, male and female, anthropologist and native, have dramatically different views of her culture and its people as well as of the nature and utility of anthropology itself.

The Smithsonian Institution Press was very helpful in the preparation of this book. Thanks are due to Daniel Goodwin of the Press and to Ivan Karp and Bill Merrill, the series editors. Bill Merrill assumed the editorial duties for this manuscript. It was most rewarding to work with an editor who understands that editing should be a dialogue between author and editor for the benefit of the reader. I should also like to thank the anonymous reviewers of the work and Rebecca Browning and Deborah Corsi of the Smithsonian Press for their comments.

Finally, a note about words. The phrase "the people" is a common translation of one of the meanings of the word *dene*. I have sometimes used it, where other phrases might be expected, in recognition of the cultural and social unity of the Chipewyan. The third person singular gender distinction in English leads to inaccurate statements of inclusion and exclusion by gender so, although it sometimes creates grammatical disharmony, I have used the third person plural where no gender exclusion is intended.

# Introduction

The major theoretical issues in this work are: (1) the nature of power in Chipewyan society; (2) the relationship between specific symbolic forms, *inkoze* and the "bushman," as a means of gender regulation; and (3) the Western concepts of "belief" and "rationality" as confounding variables in the analysis of Chipewyan thought and action.


This is a microsociological study of power, therefore a study of symbols, in interpersonal relations within a single kin group of Chipewyan in a bush camp in the Northwest Territories of Canada during the spring and summer of 1975. Studies of the nature and internal dynamics of power in such bounded kin groups in Northern Athapaskan societies are inherently significant because of the egalitarian nature of these societies. The low value the people themselves place upon seeking, holding, or exercising power is in direct contradiction to the maximization notions upon which almost all Western political (and economic) thought is based.

The most salient analyses of power in Northern Athapaskan societies have been made by MacNeish (1956), Slobodin (1969), and Ridington (1968). Ridington's analysis of the medicine fight among a related Indian group, the Beaver, shifted the focus of discussion to the processes of political action. He took a utilitarian focus "in the almost total absence of formal hierarchical political structure [to] demonstrate the possibility of a purely utilitarian political analysis. It assumes that political action can be analyzed in terms of competition for scarce and hence valuable resources as defined by the culture".

Both MacNeish and Ridington see power in terms of the ability to direct the actions of others but Ridington (1969:1153) makes two significant breaks from traditional perspectives in the analysis of Northern Athapaskan societies by recognizing that, "supernatural power forms the basis of political action," and by beginning a break from a competitive model of power.

Cohen's (1974:13) later assertion, "that the central theoretical problem in social anthropology has been the analysis of the dialectical relations between two major variables: symbolic action and power relationships", is the key step, the linking of the relationship between symbolic forms and power. Cohen's approach actualizes Fortes and Evans-Pritchard's (1940:16–22) identification of political symbols as values but is not yet an adequate conceptualization of power in Chipewyan society.

Mauss's concept of "total social phenomena" is nowhere more relevant than in the analysis of small-scale egalitarian Northern Athapaskan societies. Scale itself imposes certain requirements.[1] Our view of small-scale societies is affected by the legacy of nineteenth-century evolutionary theory, which holds that with increasing size comes increasing specialization and differentiation of institutions. "Total social phenomena" exist in societies at all points on the size–complexity scale, but among the Chipewyan there is a coherency between institutions, social practice, and culture not often attributed to larger societies. Within the coherency of Chipewyan culture, power may not be conceptualized in terms of either a zero-sum model (Von Neumann and Morganstern 1944) or a consensual model (Swartz, Turner, and Tuden 1966). Both of these approaches share the underlying assumptions of dominance models in ethology and conceptualize power as a choice between mutually exclusive options. Even though "competition" is an integral part of social relations in this culture, it is necessary to push beyond a conceptualization of power that depends upon the assumption that the ability to achieve one's goals or intentions is necessarily contingent upon control of others or denying others their goals or intentions. Where the cultural and social context within which power operates does not formulate an adversarial relationship, then the exercise of power can be devoid of the competitive and maximization notions that Western culture ascribes to it.

Native values are one of the justifications for this investigation. How is power exercised in a society hostile to its possession and exercise? The ideal answer, as a function of both scale and indigenous values, would be that power is not possessed and is not exercised, but that is not the case. Understanding the resolution of this apparent paradox rests largely upon the recognition that the Chipewyan do not see themselves as "actors." Their symbolic forms bed the individual in a matrix of causality that is external to the self; the self becomes a passive participant within a system. Causality, hence responsibility, lies beyond the self. Within this system of thought, each self acts in accordance with external forces so that all actions, even those clearly wrong or immoral, can at least be represented socially as appropriate. The Chipewyan have a strong sense of shame and guilt, therefore the social assertion of appropriateness may be matched by private feelings of doubt, blame, and responsibility. However, this social self-conceptualization of actions is crucial, for this is what negates the self-maximization notion. To view the Chipewyan as self-maximizing, in terms of economics, power, prestige, or status, is to impose upon them an analytical precondition that only distorts their actions and thought. To dispense with self-maximization as a *deus ex machina* does not, however, mean to dispense with purpose, goals, or manipulation.

The nature of Northern Athapaskan social organization has remained one of the more puzzling anthropological questions of the last half-century. Culture after culture, from Manitoba to Alaska, is described in *Subarctic*, volume six in *The Handbook of North American Indians* (Helm 1981) in essentially the same terms[2] in spite of their differences in environment, language, history, and culture. The same pattern of social organization applies to peoples described as matrilineal (with or without clans, moieties, or phratries in varying combinations), bilateral, and at least one case where the same people are either bilateral or matrilineal in different locations (Slobodin 1962). The source of this confusion has been a general failure to recognize the role of affinal kinship (Levi-Strauss 1969; Dumont 1983; Needham 1962, 1974) in organizing social groupings and the insistence that social groups of the size and nature considered here are to be fit within conventional typological frameworks (Leach 1966; Needham 1962, 1975, 1979). Typological approaches applied with some sophistication have been moderately productive (Dyen and Aberle 1974) but those of the last two decades have been largely sterile and distorting (Yerbury 1890, 1986; Bishop and Kretch 1980).

Chipewyan social groupings, in common with those of other Northern Athapaskans, are not rigid structures. These groups must be approached as polythetic categories (Needham 1962, 1975, 1978), intermediatory between the individual and the regional band (Helm and Damas 1963; Helm 1968), and delineated by the residential expression of marital alliances. Within this framework, groups such as the one discussed here are the fundamental elements of social organization.

This perspective has two immediate consequences for the conceptualization of power to be used in this work. (1) There is no distinction between "public" and "private" applicable to the exercise of power among the Chipewyan. (2) Power so permeates every social interaction among the Chipewyan that analytical maintenance of the category "political" is counterproductive. To understand the exercise of power among them it is necessary to recognize the concept of the "political" as hopelessly culture-bound and to discard it as an analytical tool.

Power, among the Chipewyan, needs to be thought of as the ability to accomplish one's own choices but without any implication that to do so necessitates control over the actions of others. It is our own view of causality and competitiveness that makes it difficult for us to see how power can mean the ability to accomplish without implying the ability to control. I shall assume that all persons and many nonhuman social figures are players in power relationships. My primary concern will be the relations between the adult men of this group, but I will examine the role women and children play. By utilizing a fluid set of categories, only partly as a product of scale, and by focusing on power rather than politics, I am able to include women and children in the analysis. I pay different kinds of attention to them, because their actions appear less problematical in Western terms than do those of the men. The dramaturgical approach will show how the power of one gender over another can be translated from symbol to action without conscious intent or recognition.

I intend to take seriously several related lines of argument that have appeared over the last fifteen years about the nature of rationality, belief, and polythetic classification; Western categories heavily utilized in anthropological work. Each will be discussed at the appropriate point in the text, but I should indicate as a prelude that I shall treat the first two as culture-bound concepts of limited applicability to the Chipewyan. The effect of these considerations will sometimes be uncomfortable, but is consonant with the position that each culture represents a separate reality that can only be interpreted rather than translated. Humanness is not an exclusive property of Western man and at times it will be necessary for the reader to grapple with the fact that even though Chipewyan behavior and thought is perfectly coherent in the context of their culture, it is not always explicable in terms of ours. To deal with "the other" it is necessary to recognize that they are "other."

As anthropology creates and reifies the modern through its search for the postmodern, ethnography itself is searching for new forms of representation that escape the limitations of the paradigm of Newtonian science. The critical assumption has been that of "human nature," an assumption necessary with a scientific metaphor. The existence of a unified human nature ought to be something that is empirically demonstrated rather than something that is assumed. Human nature has been taken as a universal human reality always partly hidden by each language and culture. The metaphor of ethnography as a process of translation between cultures has been a useful way to deal with this problem for the past few decades, but even this approach has a flaw attributable to its implicit use of science as a metaphor.

Instead of presuming each culture to represent an imperfect variation upon a broader and more basic human pattern and assuming that intelligibility between cultures will exist if only our means of communication are adequate, I choose instead to regard separate cultures as different realities of equal validity. This assumption, which is simply cultural relativism used as a methodological tool, seems to me to make the lesser of the many assumptions about human nature that anthropologists must make in order to pursue their craft. With these assumptions, the ethnographic problem becomes not one of translation from culture to culture of aspects of a single reality, but that of the interpretation between cultures of genuinely different realities.

To address this particular ethnographic situation, I shall adopt a particular role within our culture, that of a storyteller, and accomplish my interpretation through the use of a particular literary form, the narrative essay. Ethnographic representation is a form of rhetoric. The people, the events, the feel, the experiences, are not something I can share. All I can give is a verbal representation: a sharing of words. For them to make sense they must be in a form the reader finds familiar. To accomplish this, ethnographic representations are structured by theory. I shall utilize Victor Turner's (1957, 1974) concept of "social drama" as a heuristic model for my analysis. Such a quasi-dramaturgical model necessitates an intensive presentation of ethnographic data in a sequence that is primarily chronological. As my primary concern is with the expression of power in interpersonal relationships, the depth of data presentation will often approach that of descriptive social psychology.

The analysis of events is interspersed among the data, breaking at appropriate points from the narrative of what has happened into an analysis of what is happening. Consonant with the dramaturgical model, the ethnographic data will have subplots; themes of concern only to specific individuals. Among the Chipewyan, as among ourselves, knowledge is specific to individuals and cannot be assumed to be uniformly distributed. A narrative format more adequately represents the way these events were lived and provides me with the opportunity to take up a number of more limited issues than would otherwise be the case. It was fortunate that I was able to bound the presentation of these events by something more relevant than the happenstance of my arrival and departure. A sequence of events involving the diffusion of a symbolic form provided a convenient set of boundaries within the lives of the people themselves.[3]

The small group of persons examined here is quite heterogeneous but it is also a typical and representative social group. These individuals constitute nearly six percent of the total Chipewyan population in the area and are embedded in an immediate kin context that approximates twenty percent of the total population. The factors that make this group unique, other than having an attached anthropologist, in no way make them atypical or unrepresentative of the larger population.

Ethnographies are traditionally written in a hypothetical time frame called the "ethnographic present," a time that almost always seems to be just before the ethnographer arrived and the systematic nature of the culture got all fouled up by outside influences. This work can be identified with a specific time period, April to August, 1975, and subsequent representations of that time period in the summer of 1977 and the summer of 1983.

Chipewyan language and thought do not operate within an English-language time frame. The past, present, and future we project from our grammar into our "reality," and assume in the science that has become our dominant metaphor of cultural ordering, do not work well in understanding the Chipewyan. Our distinctions are often without logical meaning or social consequence in their culture. There is more to this issue than different cultural perceptions and categorical orderings of time. The individuals considered here are quite heterogeneous, both in the point at which they stand within their individual life cycles and in their depth of memory and breadth of experience. Their chronological ages range from less than two to about sixty years. Their individual experience beyond the narrow core of an ideal traditional life is equally diverse. Each of them brought to the "now" of these events very different knowledge and experience of the connections between "now" and past social and mythical life.

That the boundary between past and future in Chipewyan language and thought is of a radically different order than it is in our culture, first becomes crucial when we come to consider the supernatural (inkoze) because its atemporality is a necessary aspect of its conceptualization. When we see actions that seem scripted, the source of the script is explicable only in terms of past events and relationships that are not apparent in the contemporary situation and individual actions. These too have, on occasion, been dealt with by introducing themes, sequences of events that resonate through time and experience that are often only partly known or shared within the group.

I must end this introduction with two caveats.[4] Chipewyan life has changed drastically since 1945, and to focus upon events that occur during bush life risks catering to the stereotype that the Chipewyan are somehow unaware of the larger Canadian society in which they live. The physical isolation of bush life is the most conservative part of their culture and that most distant from Canadian society, but the notion of ignorance of the larger society is an illusion. How this stereotype can exist is illustrated by the life of one of the peripheral characters in this drama. In 1970, as a trapper, he was one of the first to tell me of the 'bushman'; in 1983, after more than a decade as an employee of a uranium mine, he chose to tell me of the safety techniques involved in handling high-grade radioactive ore. He left his job that year and returned to trapping. In his resumed life as a trapper, his knowledge of these exotic aspects of the outside world was invisible to anyone who did not already know to seek out information about it. This illusion of isolation from the larger context of their lives is deliberately created by the Chipewyan and is one of the main reasons they continue to pursue bush life.

I have chosen to conduct this investigation at a sociological rather than at a linguistic or psychological level, so the the question of "meaning" may fairly be raised. Meaning, to the natives or to the external investigator, cannot be understood in isolation from the context from which it is drawn. Conducting the examination at a sociological level assures that my explanations of their symbols will not be advanced either in terms of individual mental states or semantic relationships. There are limits to each ethnographer's skill, and I have a firm conviction from fifteen years' experience with the Chipewyan that their internal mental states and the individual meanings they draw from the symbols of their culture and the events of their lives are not to be equated with the explanations I offer. I will probe situations and events but at the level of individual meaning it is best to let the Chipewyan speak for themselves.

1. Gould (1977:171–198) is perhaps the most lucid on this topic.

2. For example: Dogrib (Helm 1981:297), Hare (Savishinsky and Hara 1981:319), Mountain (Gillespie 1981:334–335), Slavey (Asch 1981:342), Beaver (Ridington 1981:352–353), Kaska (Honigmann 1981:446–447), Tahltan (MacLachlan 1981:461), Tutchone (McClellan 1981:500), Han (Crow and Obley 1981:508), Koyukon (Clark 1981:585). Note however De Laguna and McClellan's (1981:656) comment, "Affinal relations always took precedence over the consanguineal in determining kin terms and behavior." The Chipewyan polity examined here falls well within, if toward the low side of, the classic size range of

the "band." I do not emphasize that aspect because social change and sedentarization (J. G. E. Smith 1978) in the last thirty years have removed all analytical utility from the concept below the level of the "regional band." I remain unconvinced that the concept of the local band has any utility in the analysis of postcontact Chipewyan social organization. The central role of the band in the arguments of Steward (1955) and Service (1962), and the later use of their arguments, seem to me to be without foundation. In spite of the lucidity of J. G. E. Smith's (1981:271–284) discussion of the topic, I fear the data utilized to argue the importance of the band in Chipewyan life are fatally flawed by the assumption that Chipewyan application of descriptive words or phrases to the activities or locations of temporary aggregations corresponds to English conventions of naming permanent social or residential groups (see also Helm 1981:297).

3. One process by which elements of culture, both material and intangible, spread between peoples is known as diffusion. This concept played a major role in the development of anthropology. Diffusion is a cornerstone of theory in archaeology and one of the fundamental mechanisms by which cultural similarities between peoples have been explained. From that standpoint this work is a case study of the diffusion of a symbolic form that makes a simple theoretical point: diffusion is not an explanation of what happens but a label indicating what it is that needs to be explained. In particular, the subject is the diffusion of a symbolic element of English-speaking Canadian and American culture, the Bigfoot, into the culture of an Athapaskan-speaking Indian group, the Chipewyan. These people had an existing symbolic form, known in the literature as the "bushman," that has a certain feel of similarity to the Bigfoot.

4. The issue of gender is of considerable import to this work as it is to the social sciences generally. It is best I specify my own position which is derived from both my experience of my culture and my anthropological training and experience. I have a long-standing interest in social carnivores and the role social organizations have played in the evolution of our species. My study of wolves, culture-bearing social beings that exist in a learned social system not based upon reciprocity, has led me to the conclusion that the single most important fact about human beings is that they are social. I assume the behavioral differences between human beings attributed to gender are cultural creations, unique to each culture, not explicable in terms of biological differences. Further, the existing culturally created differences among all humans are but a narrow portion of the potentially viable ways to organize a culture. The apparent cross-cultural similarity in gender roles reflects not the nature of the beast but the historical legacy of the adoption and spread of a series of very specific organizational principles during the transition from a gathering mode of living to one involving both hunting and gathering. I frequently emphasize how Chipewyan culture leads males and females to think and act differently precisely because there is no biological basis for those differences. They instead reflect the social nature of culture in its purest— and most coercive—aspect and remain one of the greatest of all sociological puzzles.

# THE TRANSFORMATION OF BIGFOOT

## THE PLAYERS

### [A] KIN RELATIONS:

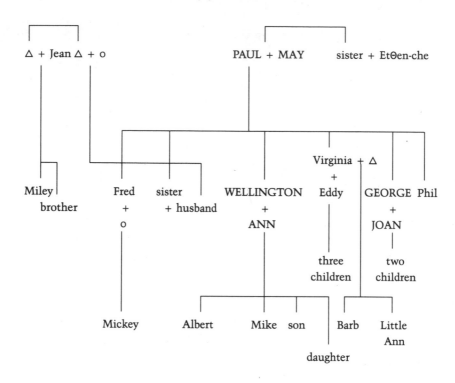

### [B] BUSH HOUSEHOLDS:

Paul and May
Mike, Barb,
little Ann,
Mickey, Phil

Jean
Miley

Wellington and Ann
Albert, small son,
infant daughter

Virginia and Eddy
infant son, two
infant daughters

George and Joan
small daughter,
infant son

Ethnographer and wife
daughter,
infant daughter

# Chapter One

Between the continuous forest belt stretching from Alaska to Maine and the sweeping tundra presaging the Arctic shore, there lies in central Canada a narrow margin of thinning forest. It is an area beset by short, cool summers and long, cold winters; temperature extremes range from more than 100 to less than – 70 degrees F. The ground is snow covered from September to May and the lakes are ice covered from October to June. The lake ice of late spring matches the snow accumulated in sheltered places; each can exceed six feet in depth, but they are both mere crusts upon the multithousand foot depths of the permafrost. Soil is sparse and acidic and summer melting reaches only a few feet into the predominant sand, far less in most places. At its southern borders the forest itself is a mixture of conifers and hardy deciduous trees. The extensive birch and aspen stands there give way farther north to widely spaced spruce with scattered birch and willow scrub along the shores. Lichen and moss provide the ground cover in undisturbed areas while sparse grasses or thick shrubs succeed where soil cover has been disturbed. Over half the surface area is either bare rock, host to a scale of almost microscopic growth, or standing water in lake, muskeg, and stream.

This thin belt of transitional forest, rarely a hundred miles in width, was center stage of traditional Chipewyan life. In this homeland east of Great Slave Lake there is easy access to the characteristic flora and fauna of both tundra and boreal forest proper. This harsh land of brutal extremes provided a security of livelihood, to those hardy and wise enough to understand it, that was often greater than that afforded by milder and richer lands far to the south. The Chipewyan held this land as the quintessential hunters of large game, their diet approximating ninety percent animal tissue. In his journal entries for March,

1771, the first European to enter their homeland, Samuel Hearne (1971:82–83), wrote:

> It is undoubtedly the duty of every one of the Company's servants to encourage a spirit of industry among the natives, and to use every means in their power to induce them to procure furrs [sic] and other commodities for trade, by assuring them of a ready purchase and good payment for everything they bring to the Factory: and I can truly say, that this has ever been the grand object of my attention. But I must at the same time confess, that such conduct is by no means for the real benefit of the poor Indians; it being well known that those who have the least intercourse with the Factories, are by far the happiest. As their whole aim is to procure a comfortable subsistence, they take the most prudent methods to accomplish it; and by always following the lead of the deer, are seldom exposed to the griping hand of famine, so frequently felt by those who are called the annual traders.

Public and anthropological awareness of the Chipewyan suffers from the similarity of their English name to that of the Chippewa, a more numerous and better known Indian people living hundreds of miles to the southeast. Even anthropologists often confuse the two, politely assuming any reference to the Chipewyan is either a misspelling or mispronunciation of Chippewa. It is only within the last fifteen years that a significant body of ethnographic works have appeared on the Chipewyan. These studies, along with those flowing from the growing ethnohistorical interest in the postcontact Canadian Athapaskans, have made a sufficient body of ethnographic data readily available so that I need provide here only a brief summary suitable to locate them in a cultural context. I have included a number of the major ethnographic works in the bibliography for the convenience of readers not familiar with this part of the world.

The picture of Chipewyan prehistory is not clear, but they seem to be descendants of late migrants from Asia. Their homeland was locked in the glacial freeze until nearly 12,000 years ago, therefore human (re)occupation was late.[1] They are probably descendants of a people who moved into the region 1,500 to 2,000 years before post-Viking Europeans reached North America. There is no possible way the Chipewyan could have avoided becoming entangled in the changes resulting from post-Viking European settlement. The entire continent was wrapped in turmoil from the continuing European increase that spread inland from the coastal areas of the east, south, and west. Contact came through those perpetual handmaidens of change: trade and war. Its nature and effects are much debated and its timing uncertain (Yerbury 1980, 1986; J. G. E. Smith 1975, 1976; Gillespie 1975; Wolf 1982).

The subjects of our tale, the "Caribou-Eater" Chipewyan (J. G. E. Smith 1975) remained longest in these ancestral areas in pursuit of Hearne's "deer," the barren ground caribou (*Rangifer tarandus groenlandicus*) (Banfield 1961). They were affected by Europeans later and at a slower pace than were their southern neighbors. At all times their dealings with whites have been dominated by two factors: (1) their homeland is not suitable for any known form of agriculture and (2) no European derived form of social organization is able to sustain itself here without extensive involvement with and dependency upon outside resources.

These points are a major factor in contemporary Chipewyan identity and style of life. Their land is an anathema to their southern Canadian contemporaries. It is empty, harsh, cold, and almost devoid of marketable resources. Its timber is too small to harvest, its fish too far from market, its people consume little, and there is nothing to tax; it cannot be settled, farmed, or herded. What white Canadians coming here think about the place soon becomes what they feel about its native inhabitants. In anathema there is ambivalence. The vast "Great White North" is the seat of the deepest dreams of Canadian power and wealth: if only it could be tapped for its riches. Many Canadians come to the north for wealth and adventure, others are sent there on hardship tours to gain experience or for punishment. Many come, most soon fear and hate it. They mine it, exploit it, administer it, and leave.

To the Chipewyan the land and its native life forms are life itself. It is their home.

After contact with the fur traders, the Chipewyan shifted their area of exploitation to the South and Southwest. Whether this constitutes an expansion into new areas as Gillespie (1975) seems to see it or as a withdrawal from old areas, as I think Smith and Burch see it, is as yet unresolved. Those Chipewyan who moved to new areas where fur-bearing animals were more common but barren ground caribou were scarcer or absent had to make major adjustments to

their economic and subsistence systems. The apparent stability of
the nineteenth century began to break down in the first part of the
twentieth century (Helm and Damas 1963; Helm et al. 1975). A treaty
was signed with the Canadian government around the turn of the
century but had little immediate impact. It was World War I and its
aftermath that laid the groundwork for major change by bringing
white trappers into the area. These trappers were the first Europeans
in Chipewyan history to live in significant numbers among them
out in the bush. They brought intermarriage and increased exposure
to Canadian culture. A Hudson's Bay Company store was established
in the study area in the 1920s to counter the more sophisticated mar-
keting techniques of the white trappers and to challenge the resur-
gent operation of free traders.

The Chipewyan population was beginning to recover from its losses
in the flu pandemic of 1918–1919, which they estimate to have killed
between seventy and eighty of the people, when the white trappers
began to arrive. The epidemic, dated by life cycles, happened early
here, before 1920. The real basis of social change would prove to result
not from the epidemic but from the increased hunting pressure on
the caribou herds that came with the influx of the white population.
The white trappers specialized by type of fur and local environmental conditions. They spaced themselves throughout the entire range
of the Mission people and extended out onto the barren grounds far
beyond any recent Chipewyan usage. Their influx more than dou-
bled the number of active trappers.

The Chipewyan themselves are heavy users of caribou. Security
in this land comes in the form of caribou killed and ready for use so
one always kills more rather than less. It is easier to survive wasting
caribou through excess killing than it is to survive a lack of food
from killing too few. The whites, aside from feeding themselves, their
dependents, and their sled dogs, used large numbers of caribou for
bait. It was hardly uncommon to kill caribou and let them rot to
attract fur-bearing animals. It was common to spread poison over
vast areas to catch fox and wage Western man's idiotic holy war
against the wolf. Each poison bait required at least part of a caribou
carcass. The additional presence of thirty to fifty white trappers and
their dependents for over two decades, a rapidly growing Chipewyan
population, and a greatly increased number of sled dogs (J. G. E. Smith

1981) brought devastation to the caribou herds. World War II drew most of the whites out for the war effort but the damage had been done. By the end of the war, in no case later than the end of the decade, the caribou had been reduced from their earlier two and one-half million animals to slightly more than one-quarter million animals.

The Chipewyan have endured declines in the caribou herds before. Burch (1977:142) identifies at least one lengthy one in the period 1830 to 1850, but this time they were able to deal with the decline by drawing upon the resources of the larger Canadian economy. In other places the Canadian government relocated whole Chipewyan bands, ostensibly out of fears they would starve, but wage labor and high fur prices within the study area allowed the Chipewyan to make greater use of commercial foodstuffs and the ecological diversity of the total area of exploitation prevented famine. With the collapse of the postwar boom in fur prices, hungry Chipewyan were forced to spend a large part of the year out of the bush and became a "problem" for the federal and provincial governments.

The 1950s saw the Chipewyan make the basic transition from a bush dwelling subsistence economy based upon hunting, trapping, and fishing with a quasi-nomadic pattern of dispersal throughout their territory to a semisedentary village economy (J. G. E. Smith 1970, 1976, 1978; D. M. Smith 1982; Van Stone 1965). The bush remained paramount in terms of subsistence, but in a reversal of orientation became a place where one went rather than where one lived. The base of operations became the village with its store where an increasing cash income was garnered through wage labor and government payments. This transition also meant a changing way of using the land and relating to possessions. Before, the Chipewyan were extremely mobile, often changing camps thirty or more times a year, but village life reduced this pattern of movement. The decreased Chipewyan reliance upon mobility as a survival strategy allowed the accumulation of goods, especially heavy and luxury goods, as there was no longer the same need either to transport them with every move or to abandon them. Adoption of a village life style created certain problems that had been minimized by the earlier mobile life style. The village in my study, which I have named Mission, is at the extreme southern edge of the transitional forest along the same

-20°F mean January isotherm as Fairbanks, Alaska and is within an area of discontinuous permafrost, with all that implies for slow growth of vegetation, slow rates of biological decay, slow growth rates of fish and animal life, and slow purging of contaminants and pollution. Earlier, the Chipewyan had intensively used an area of ground for a short time and then abandoned it, often for more than a human life span. Village life demands a Euro-Canadian pattern of continuous occupancy of a single piece of ground, a pattern whose long range viability is uncertain simply for reasons of sanitation (Chang 1962; Helm 1981:664–665; J. G. E. Smith 1978).

As the Chipewyan came to spend a large part of each year in the village, a division between those who went into the Northwest Territories to hunt and trap and those who remained within the provincial boundaries began to widen. Traplines were registered and conservation districts formed within the province as a means of excluding white trappers and allowing the local populations of beaver and other fur-bearers to recover. This marginally reduced Chipewyan mobility. They could not legally trap in areas where they were not registered, and game regulations in the province and in the Northwest Territories are supposed to prevent individuals from hunting in both jurisdictions. The total area of exploitation is a roughly north–south corridor up to 175 miles by 250 miles and approaches 50,000 square miles. With a population of less than 850 people it is too large to be effectively policed. In practice, regulations are applied only to the sale of fur, which can be monitored by making export and transportation permits a requirement for its sale at fur auctions in the South.

Those Chipewyan licensed and registered to hunt and trap south of the village do not range out as far as the northerners. Population density in the bush to the south is higher than that to the north and brings greater contact with Chipewyan from other villages and those Chipewyan living along the Churchill River system in particular. Basing their families in the town while the men went off alone had a number of advantages. This pattern began to emerge shortly after the local population was staggered by the measles epidemic of 1948 that killed over forty people. Staying in the village was easier on the women and children at a time when caribou were scarce and bush life, hard. The availability of some health care at a clinic staffed by a nurse was important. Families that remained in the village had year-round access to ration payments, a welfare obligation of the federal government perceived by the local Chipewyan as a treaty right. They were then paid only in the form of credit at the Hudson's Bay Company store in the village. The furs taken from their traplines could be sold after each run of the line and generally involved small numbers of furs and minor amounts of money. These sales were rarely reported to the Indian Agent by the manager of the Hudson's Bay Company store at Mission, therefore the amount of the sale was not deducted from the monthly ration payment. Reporting these sales to Indian Affairs, as was required, would have decreased the amount of each trapper's income from rations and the store's volume of business. The store manager's yearly bonus was figured as a percentage of the increase in the annual volume of the store's business, hence this practice allowed the southern Chipewyan to receive the full benefit of both the ration system and their fur sales.

The northern group went into the Northwest Territories in mid- to late summer and remained there until Easter. Coming into the village only for the Christmas season, they would return to the bush well before the spring caribou migration. They hunted and trapped too far from the village to leave their families there, as to do so meant not seeing them for months at a time—risky business for a married man worried about his spouse's fidelity—and the families would be denied the caribou meat that was the staple element of the northerner's diet. Some of them were just beginning to leave their families in town in 1969–1970. The late summer to late spring exploitation of the bush diminished to the months of the fall caribou migration on through to Christmas. In 1969 there were roughly 170 people in the Northwest Territories for the fall migration and trapping season. By 1975, partly in response to declining fur prices, there were only forty to fifty there and most of them were men. Even this limited continuation of this pattern of life came from a stronger attachment to traditional values and a different idea of where home truly was.

Between 1969, when my study began, and 1975, a number of major changes occurred in the conditions of village life. A housing program instituted in 1965 added eight western-style houses each year and its cumulative impact disrupted traditional patterns of residence. In the summer of 1970 the village was wired for electricity and generators were put in (the small resident white community had long had electricity and plumbing). Live electric service allowed the use of a wider range of products than did batteries and appliances were cheaper to purchase and operate. Electricity generated a flood of contact with the outside world.

Wages were low in 1969. The two major jobs, fighting fires or guiding for tourist fishermen, were seasonal and paid only eight dollars for a twelve-hour day. There were less than five year-round jobs available to Indians in a community nearing five hundred people. By 1972 the situation had begun to change rapidly. The number of year-round jobs was up markedly and pay scales had increased nearly fifty percent for the staple summer jobs while the vicious inflationary spiral induced by the various oil crises had not yet begun to raise the cost of living. There were about twenty snowmobiles in the village that year as well as several cars and trucks. There had been but a single operating example of each in the winter of 1969–1970. Funds for these purchases came mostly from federal training programs or make-work jobs, but the presence of Canada Manpower Upgrading programs in particular represented a major change. They paid a salary to take courses designed to improve skills saleable in the job market. The programs were open to both men and women and were the first opportunity many women had to have an earned income. Funding for these programs did not seem unrelated to the federal government's desire to get this group of Chipewyan to agree to fixed reserve boundaries. The general trend of prosperity continued through 1975. Jobs were available almost on demand for younger English-speaking men throughout most of the year. A good many individuals were earning cash incomes in excess of $1,000 a month, and these were largely disposable incomes because of the minimal cost of housing and the high percentage of subsistence that still came from the bush. The extent to which income had increased in the village could be seen in the presence of 80 to 100 snowmobiles, each costing a minimum of $725 at the Hudson's Bay Company store. The store's volume of business was up from well under $200,000 a year in 1969–1970 to about $500,000 for 1974–1975.

1. I hold a somewhat radical view on this topic. I am unable to see any good reason why human occupation of North America should not have occurred at least 200,000 B.P. It is not a question of existing evidence for a human occupation but a question of how to interpret the behavioral potential of our ancestors. I doubt that physical conditions that could not stop other mammalian immigrants would have stopped our ancestors. By the same token, I think it likely that the areas occupied by the Chipewyan were settled prior to the onset of the last glaciation, but it is unlikely that any discernible evidence of habitation would have survived.

# Chapter Two

In the summer of 1974, Paul and May brought their young grandson
Mike to visit me in Vancouver. I knew them well from 1969–1970 but
did not see much of them in 1972. I hoped to stay with them during
my next field trip as I had only lived in the bush for two months
during my fieldwork and wished to spend more time observing that
aspect of Chipewyan life. In the course of a pleasant visit we agreed
to spend the following spring, summer, and fall, at Foxholm Lake in
the Northwest Territories where Paul had built a cabin in 1970. I had
spent part of July, August, and September of 1970 there and was
pleased by the choice. I assumed all the social arrangements were
made and that some other family members would join us for the
sojourn up north.

I made preparations throughout the fall and winter and arranged
for the purchase and shipment of supplies and equipment which
would arrive at various times between April and June as the transport systems began to function with the coming of spring. Putting
together a field trip is a nightmare because, on top of everything else,
it is always undercapitalized. Even with a research grant, one has to
dig deeply into one's own pocket. Preparations more or less complete,
my wife and two daughters left for the village at the end of March
while I remained behind a week or so to finish the semester's grading. I arrived in the village in early April, planning to start into the
Northwest Territories after no more than a week. As far south as the
village is located, the ice conditions deteriorate quickly in the spring.
I did not wish to add the hazards of bad ice to an already difficult
overland trek.

The central focus of Chipewyan life has been pursuit of the barren ground caribou, and their relationship with the environment has
been structured by their culture's historical concentration upon this

species as the primary food source. Throughout the fur trade, caribou always came first; trade, raiding, and trapping were secondary activities. In the early history of this village that orientation to caribou remained, but in the 1970s new orientations were beginning to rival it in economic if not moral terms. Paul and May's children were no exception to these trends. Paul and May themselves remained focused upon the caribou as did their youngest adult son George and one of their married daughters. Their oldest son Fred abandoned bush life shortly after being widowed and now worked at a mine as a heavy-equipment operator. Two other daughters had abandoned bush life entirely except for holidays. The source of contention lay in their second son Wellington. He retained an orientation toward bush life but was ceasing to see it in the traditional terms of a source of a subsistence existence with a minor cash income from trapping. He was aware of the economic possibilities of the tourist trade and had developed the ambition to own his own fish camp.

Between my previous departure in January, 1973, and return in April of 1975, changes in the economic structure of the village affected the fieldwork in unanticipated ways. The increase in income and the availability of jobs had drawn much more of the community into year-round village life. Spending months in the bush was fast becoming a separate occupational specialty rather than the normal pattern. I could not tell until after the fact, but these changes had begun to alter the plans even before I left for the field. What I had thought a firm plan to go to Foxholm Lake had become an issue of contention.

All during the week we prepared for the journey there was a running discussion of where we were to go. I preferred to go to Foxholm Lake but did not wish to impose my views. If for no other reason, the less "unnatural" my being there made the situation, the better it was for my purposes. Paul and May wanted to go to Foxholm Lake but took their own preference as secondary to avoiding conflict in the family. George preferred the physical environment of Foxholm Lake but there was a degree of ambivalence on his part. Wellington had a compelling economic argument for another place, South Lake, where the fly-in fish camp he wished to purchase was located. As he presented the situation, he was waiting approval from Indian Affairs for an interest-free loan to purchase the camp. If Wellington owned the camp, he could offer George summer employment and he held out

the possibility of an income from guiding fishermen even if he did
not obtain ownership. It was this set of arguments that got my assent
for South Lake. I knew George was passing up his normal summer
wage labor in order to be in the bush with his parents and my family.
I was reluctant to be the reason for further economic loss by insist-
ing upon another lake where there was no possibility of a cash income.
The idea of their earning a living from bush employment in the company of their families was an intriguing notion. Once I agreed to South
Lake the issue was decided.

In the complex interactions of fieldwork it is often difficult to
remember that acting to avoid introducing change is itself an action,
one that may serve only to introduce change in less desirable ways.
The decision not to act by one's normal motivation leads to actions
based on an exterior code constructed from one's ideas about what
the situation and culture should be rather than one's observations of
what they are. This influx of a private moral aesthetic increases the
difficulty informants have in trying to understand and deal with you.
In the ensuing events I was already a precipitating factor, as it is
unlikely these people would have spent so much time in the bush
that spring if I had not been there. Even if they had, they would not
have done so with quite the same clustering of people. As an external person I was wrong to think there was any way that I could
have avoided being maneuvered into expressing a position and taking responsibility for the choice of location. The ethnologist's social
position is often assigned rather than achieved and actions to avoid
its consequences only produce different results rather than better
ones.

Chipewyan social life in villages or other high-density residential
situations is based upon individual social ties structured by relationships of kinship and marriage. In these high-density situations it is
the relationships among members of each individual's separate kindred that provide the primary pathways of social interaction. To leave
a high-density residential situation for the isolation of bush life
requires a drawing together of persons of different categories so as to
produce a subsistence unit capable of feeding itself in isolation. These
subsistence groups can exist only in social isolation from the over-
whelming abundance of structured relationships provided by each
individual's kindred.[1] A core grouping of one of these subsistence units,

such as the one formed around Paul and May, can exist for years, but each time it goes into isolation it faces the problem of recruiting members. This particular occurrence was in many ways typical of the process. A set of people who shared an intent to go to the bush in a particular time frame, within a general area, and for similar purposes, had already sorted itself out from a larger set of possible members. What was not resolved by the time of my arrival were questions of the specifics of location and membership. Hovering behind these questions were more subtle ones of power, authority, and leadership in the forming group.

I should be less than honest if I said I did not anticipate a crisis in the relationship between George and Wellington. I had known both of them for five years and the factors leading to it were clear. The pending crisis was a major reason I came to the field a year earlier than originally planned. I was, however, less than fully aware of the seriousness of the major nonstructural issue involved in changing these peoples' relationships. Paul had suffered a heart attack a few years before, and during the visit to Vancouver was diagnosed as having emphysema. He no longer had the stamina bush life required to live apart from other adult males.

Once Paul and George committed themselves to go where I went, the situation forced a claim to leadership upon Wellington. He had previously demonstrated his independence by living alone with his family for extended periods, something George had not done, keeping his family instead either in the camp of his parents or his parents-in-law. South Lake was where Wellington had moved to etablish his independence and had chosen as his base area rather than his father's, even though it was only twenty air miles away from Foxholm Lake and Paul had trapped and hunted there throughout his life. Getting me to go South Lake, thereby drawing his father and brother to a place that was, as it were, his own turf was itself a claim to influence. What made his actions an inescapable claim to leadership was his announced intention of having his widowed mother-in-law and her two grown, unmarried sons spend June through December there. It was not simply being at South Lake, for they all had spent the fall of 1974 there, that made Wellington's claim, but the social factors related to his aggregating other people around him, his potential control of the fish camp, and his father's declining health.

I don't wish to compound a possibly confusing situation by allowing a shadow of the history of Algonquin ethnography raise what is a dead issue in Northern Athapaskan ethnography, the ownership of land, places, or wildlife. The concept of ownership is simply not applicable. By "places" I mean specific locations for setting a few tents or building cabins, not control of resources in the bush surrounding the camp sites. Even traplines reflect preferences for types of animals to trap, amounts of timber versus open ground, number and nature of watercourses, supernatural relationships, and aesthetics rather than the control of resources.

## May

May was born in 1919 in one of the southern communities that were a product of Chipewyan expansion. She was the youngest of a large family and had not been to her birthplace since childhood. She was not to manage that trip until the late 1970s. At this time she was not certain if all of her siblings still survived and was reluctant to speak about them. The history of Chipewyan-white contact there is quite different from that in the area she now calls home, differences that are reflected in her life history. Her favorite story of her family was a romantic tale of the marriage of her grandfather. A local store owner, reputed to be of the Scottish persuasion, announced to the world at large that his daughter was ready for marriage. He would give her to the first man to appear at his store on the appointed day. May's grandfather previously had been smitten by this girl. Hearing of her father's words, he left home several days before the appointed date and camped on the store owner's door. Whether or not the man had been serious about the disposition of his daughter, the earnestness of the young man impressed him and the marriage of the two was arranged.

May's parents were involved in a small farm and store but lost their ability to make a living from them during the depression. Like many of the people of that area similarly affected, they moved north to the Chipewyan homeland to take up a bush-trapping life style among the caribou herds. They took May, just entering her teens, two of her elder sisters and an elder brother. The rest of their children were either married or otherwise too settled to move. Her two sisters subsequently married white trappers and May spent much of her early adulthood in the company of these men. During this period she gained a strong command of English; for years she and her siblings were among the best native speakers of English in the area. She also acquired a smashed knee in an ice-skating accident that left her partially crippled.

Her father was, according to family stories, quite accomplished in *inkoze* (sorcery) and her mother was an accomplished midwife. From this early exposure to *inkoze* May has adopted a hostile and disbelieving stance toward anything relating to it, yet she displays more fear at any manifestation of it than any other Chipewyan woman I know. In the time I have known her, her belief in religion has hardened into an ambivalent bitterness toward injustice, with her perception that the Chipewyan receive far more than is their due.

May is not a big woman. Standing no more than five foot three inches, she has had many health problems and presents an image of almost frothy insubstantiality and fragility. She is in fact an extremely vigorous and remarkably durable individual who has survived troubles that by rights should have killed her several times over. She, like many Chipewyan women, prides herself on her verbal aggressiveness, "I could say anything." Her skill at translating had made her among the most frequently called upon of all native interpreters. To avoid using the priest on matters of sensitivity or where the church's position was suspect, she would often be the only woman present at otherwise all-male meetings with all-male parties of outsiders. It was never apparent to the outsiders and only rarely to the Chipewyan that the view she presented to the outside world was often hers rather than an accurate translation of the men's statements. The relationship between women and public power is rarely as one-sided as it sometimes seems fashionable to assert.

It is harder for me to guess what May was like before I arrived in the field than to guess what Paul was like; perhaps because I know her so much better than I do him. As she was throughout her fifties, when I first knew her, she was not an easy woman to understand. Perhaps coming to know someone only means learning to tolerate their paradoxes and contradictions. May was intelligent, determined, and almost iron-willed at times. She could be abrasive past the point of abusiveness. When her quick and awesome temper showed, it could dominate an entire camp of her kin and affines for hours on end. She was generally cheerful and good-natured but always a pensiveness marked by a deep and dark streak of fatalism lurked nearby. For all her potential for rage, she was the adult source of affection, consolation, and sympathy when her children were small. If her affection was tempered with anger and her sympathy somewhat uncertain, her patience was monumental. She, however grudgingly, was there when truly needed if not always when desired. Never have I known a person less obtrusively generous than she was to those family and kin with a genuine claim upon her.

May is a moral woman and her strong belief in the rightness of certain courses of action have brought her and her children a pain whose cause she does not clearly perceive and that she is helpless to change. Part of the contrast between the distinct personalities of her and her husband is one of simple socialness. Paul only came into the full richness of himself as he entered the bush, while May was a person of other people who lost a part of herself those rare times she was alone.

Wellington's father-in-law had been taken south to a mental hospital nearly twenty years before. The stories I gathered about his illness either attributed it to incorrectly performed dog magic or having slept on some unmarked graves while returning home from the bush. The latter act resulted in the ghosts of the dead driving him insane. When he was taken out to the hospital, leaving his wife with three young children to raise, the hospital authorities did not notify his family of his fate or future prospects. For seventeen years his family had no idea as to his whereabouts or if he were alive.[2] His family was reduced to extreme poverty, and his children grew up under conditions that were harsh even by the Chipewyan standards of the time. After he reached retirement age, he began to draw a pension while he was still in the hospital. With a lack of information about his dependents hospital authorities deposited the checks in a bank account. As his death became imminent, concern arose over the disposition of his future estate. Inquiries resulted in the discovery of his family, and they were notified that he still lived and of the existence of the estate to be. His sons went to visit him shortly before he died, but his wife refused to make the trip. When we went into the bush his family had become heirs to an estate of some $7,000. This was an unheard of amount in the local experience and his sons were anxiously awaiting its arrival.

To a person with Wellington's hopes and dreams, his brothers-in-law were a resource whose cultivation could do much to ensure the success of his planned ventures. He was not after their money, had no direct interest in the money, no claim to it, and to my knowledge made no claim on it, but saw their having it as something that could help create a situation in which he and his kin could live in the bush together and be able to earn a living there. He foresaw, correctly, that left to their own devices his brothers-in-law would rapidly fritter it away. These two men were curious lads, pleasant and almost innocuous but with reputations for marginality. They remained unmarried, keeping them from full adult male status. One was in his late twenties and had the remarkable reputation of simultaneously being a sexual deviant and a virgin. I have great appreciation for the other one, Miley, as he is the only adult male Chipewyan I know whose sense of direction is worse than my own.

I did not realize it at the time, or rather was too busy to pay attention to it, but both May and George had intuitively recognized the implications of the situation. They wished to avoid it by going to Foxholm Lake but their only real course of action, without provoking conflict, was to manipulate me into going to Foxholm Lake. Lest this all sound too Machiavellian, I should indicate that all this maneuvering was conducted through constant talk and was very low key. The choice of a location was only one of many concerns about the trip and its arrangements that were being simultaneously negotiated.

Chipewyan leadership falls roughly within the picture presented by MacNeish (1956). Leadership is informal and conducted by example rather than direction (D. M. Smith 1982), so my use of the word "claim" above needs clarification. Wellington's claim was never voiced or stated and may never have been a conscious consideration in his or anyone else's mind but mine. There is no formal position or office to occupy, there is only gathering people around yourself and having them tend to follow your lead and take your advice. What was at stake was a question of influence, not one of authority. Wellington was doing this regardless of whether or not it was his intention to do so. He knew that my decision, at a time when I was trying hard not to make one and alter the "natural" situation, was the key to his being able to do what he wanted to do in the company of his kin rather than away from them. By making a direct economic case to me, largely through third parties, he hit closer to my own values as a member of Western culture than did the other three persons making competing cases. Their cases, again made through third persons, were more in terms of their own values. They did not so closely parallel Western values and were less effective in maneuvering me.

The processes by which a decision was reached were typical. There was a continuous, if intermittent, flow of discussion between all of the adults. Argumentation never took the form of direct confrontation, and as individual positions and concerns emerged, discussion was directed to third persons who would carry each speaker's point of view back to others with different views. The underlying subject — redefinition of relationships among the men — was never discussed. Location, with its implications for earned cash income and a shift in Wellington's influence, came to be the twice-removed subject through which a decision would be reached. Shifting the decision to me allowed responsibility for the immediate consequences of the ultimate decision to be displaced onto a person of more distant relationship. It was easier for Paul, May, and George to agree to do what I wished to do than to face directly the implications of internal redefinition.

Wellington had committed himself to going to South Lake to be near the fish camp. For him the question was whether or not he was to be in isolation or with his kin. Paul and George were the ones at risk from an error in judgment. Paul risked the splintering of his sons and consequent dependency without them to offset each other, while George risked his ability to establish his own identity as an independent player if he fell into a subordinate role vis-à-vis his elder brother.

During the first days of my stay in Mission, I received a visit from an old friend, known often as the Old Black Woman because the sun and wind had tanned her so darkly. She and her husband, both in their seventies, had been among the first Chipewyan to take kindly to me, and I had my first conversation in Chipewyan with him. Her visit was serious. She had been out to the university hospital for treatment and had just returned. I do not know what was wrong; she had gone out because she was unable to keep any food down, but their treatment had not helped. She had come to me for medicine, as she feared she would starve to death. What she wanted was *nydie*, medicine with a supernatural basis of action. I knew what she was seeking and that I could provide her with a harmless concoction that might assuage her fears if not her symptoms, but my own fear of claiming the status of a healer by supernatural means—and the fear of ridicule if I tried and failed—kept me from venturing a cure. I turned instead to the supply of patent medicines I had with me, but she had tried all of them. I have yet to escape entirely the guilt that has come from my unwillingness to appear foolish.

The following week we were able to start people and supplies off to South Lake. The men arranged the rental of aircraft to take supplies, women and children, and some of the dogs. Paul was unable to make the trip by land and his dogs could not even if he could. No one liked the idea of the women and children arriving so long before the men, so he went along with them. He would be able to kill caribou if the spring migration had reached the lake. After all, the main reason for going now rather than after the ice had melted in June was to make dry caribou meat. On Monday, Paul and May and their dependents, Wellington's wife and children, my wife and children, and George's wife and children flew out. George and I left the following Friday, with Wellington scheduled to follow a day later.

We finished loading by 9:30 A.M. and were about ready to depart, but a mutual friend, who had said he intended to travel part way with us, hadn't shown up yet. George was unconcerned and ready to leave without him, but I was worried he might show up late, find us gone, and be offended. George's assessment of the situation was better than mine. We found that our friend had fallen victim to a party the night before, and an invigorating snowmobile trip is not "a hair of the dog that bit you." All the while we were loading, neighbors stopped by to offer advice about the trip, check our loading and balance, and give us the latest word on trail conditions. George's dog team was carrying most of the lighter supplies, including all the food and bedding. I had Paul's toboggan to pull behind the snowmobile, and it was loaded with the heavier items and thirty-five gallons of gasoline. We departed at 1:30 P.M. amid concern over the state of the trails.

The area around the village is heavily exploited and the lake is the main pathway for that exploitation. Summer and winter it is a highway to every point along its shore. Leaving the lake and moving into the surrounding bush by any form of transportation other than shank's mare means being constrained by a set of trail networks developed over the years in accord with changing Chipewyan needs for movement. Primary egress to the north is via a single trail developed out of what was the major canoe route between the stores in the south and Missionary Lake in the Northwest Territories. That trail evolved under the constraints of making the most effective use of water courses to minimize packing, loading, unloading, and distance. This trail is not particularly suited for travel by dog team and even less so by snowmobile. Both are better able to utilize low-lying ground through frozen muskegs, along stream courses, and sheltered lake shores. Snowmobiles are now the primary traffic on the trail, but they are so fast that it has been easier to keep using the existing trails known to everyone than to break a new set.

We spent Saturday and Sunday nights in a bush settlement of indeterminate antiquity. Hearne (1971) passed north of here on his epic journey to the Arctic Ocean in the 1770s and found, within the present day range of these people, a substantial camp with indications that others were in the area. Nomenclature may be a problem here, as Chipewyan villages (camps, settlements) do not stay in the same place, contain the same people, or necessarily exist continuously for even a season, yet they remain the same. Like traveling carnivals or fairs, they are always different but always the same. This village is relocated every few years as trash builds up and local supplies of wood, small game, and fish are depleted. The current village was built between 1970 and 1972, by which time it had over one hundred inhabitants. I visited it in late fall 1972 and was struck by the ruddy good health of everyone and the cleanliness and cheerfulness of the place (even if an untethered team of sled dogs did try to eat me just because I attempted to take their picture). In 1975, it was reduced to eight cabins in various states of disrepair. Only three were to be used that fall. George pointed out to me the home of the Old Black Woman and gave me a particularly extensive tour of her cabin. The village had become notorious the last few years for the indolence of its inhabitants. Instead of seriously hunting and fishing, they settled in and fished haphazardly until the caribou came. They then hunted a bit, making only a little dry meat. Many of the men no longer bothered to set a trapline and some of them set four or five lines in such a way that the men could take turns running them, a practice abhorrent to a traditionalist. Rented high-frequency radios allowed a nightly stream of chatter between here and the main village, eliminating worry about kin left behind in the south. The people stay until the easily accessible caribou are gone and then go into the main village for Christmas.

## George

George was in his late twenties in 1975. Youngest of the middle set of Paul and May's children, he was five years younger than Wellington. Children in Chipewyan families do not spend their youth in the same kind of residential pattern that is the ideal in our own society. Many live for extended periods with other relatives and may be weeks or months away from their parents. As a boy, George lived for a few years with his paternal grandparents, as had Fred. During his teens he spent most of each year for seven years with his aunt and EtΘen-che, the man who lived with her. This was a seasonal pattern that began as a training process and ended when it did not transform into an adequately paid employee relationship. During these years with EtΘen-che he mastered the skills of bush life and discovered that he had a strong preference for the Chipewyan approach to the bush and its wildlife. This preference for the Chipewyan way had survived an earlier stint in a Catholic boarding school that constituted his only formal schooling. George left EtΘen-che in the summer of 1970 while I was with his parents at Foxholm Lake. He remained with his parents and quickly established his identity as an eligible bachelor.

Standing between five foot seven and five foot nine, he is the smallest male in his family, already equaled in height by his then fourteen-year-old brother, Phil. George is thin but well muscled rather than wiry, his strong suit is endurance rather than strength. Small size and light weight are often useful in this environment where men spend so much time moving over crusted snow and thin ice. He was often able to move freely in circumstances where Wellington or I found ourselves immobilized. George's greatest social asset is his sense of humor and an almost unfailing delight in the natural and social world around him, but he lacks the keen intelligence of Paul and Wellington and the questioning nature of his father. Capable of bursts of anger that are more like tantrums than rage, he is best characterized by his almost gentle searching for humor—an expression of his basic temperament rather than the control over emotion that is the hallmark of Paul. He was often embarrassingly transparent and this created in him a vulnerability frequently used by stronger or more selfish personalities around him.

By the end of the day Wellington had not come so we prepared to depart in the morning. From the time we reached the south shore of Stop Lake, changes in the environment occurred at an accelerating pace. One lake shore could be in full boreal forest seemingly indistinguishable from northern Maine, while the other shore showed dramatic portents of the awaiting tundra. As the tree line approaches the hardwoods vanish from the forest and the trees become more widely spaced, much like the dry cedar forests of the American West. As the space between trees increases the ability of forest fires to sustain themselves decreases. Individual trees are exposed to less risk and there is a dramatic increase in their size. Brooding giants are often found a few dozen yards from gnarled and stunted dwarves that grow less than a foot a decade. The undergrowth, a void of shrubs and the frenetic growth of intruding grasses, creates a manicured lichen garden of subtle hues and textures. Hillsides are capped with tundra patches stretching for miles before vanishing into a distant lake or stand of trees that emerges from some hidden gully whose depth gave them shelter from the north wind as they first clawed their way toward the sky. The tree line drops closer and closer to its goal of sea level; what takes 12,000 feet of elevation to accomplish in the Sangre de Cristos is here accomplished in a scant hundred.

We passed a cabin at the south end of Stop Lake and continued on to Paul's old camp at its north end. He had placed this camp near one of the few real rivers in the whole region and we had to exercise care from here on, as the condition of the ice became increasingly uncertain. This camp was last used in 1972 and both Paul and Wellington had cabins here. George was newly married that year and had only a tiny cabin hastily thrown together as a place of seclusion in his bachelor days. Wellington had moved over to South Lake in 1973 and both he and his father had left things behind, intending soon to camp here again. The intervening two years had been hard on the perishables, as squirrels and mice moved into the cabins. Small animals can become quite possessive of abandoned cabins. When we moved later that year to Foxholm Lake a marmot, which had taken up residence under a corner of George's cabin, refused for almost a week to abandon its home to the children, dogs, noise, and bustle of our coming.

Paul was born near here and two of his and May's infant children lie buried atop the esker that overlooks the river. He has cabins scattered in an arc from here to sixty miles northwest. In the course of a lifetime a man builds up a string of dwellings that are known and secure stopping places throughout his favored living areas. I had seen this camp in 1972 on the same trip I made to the bush village and was struck here not so much by the cleanliness and sheer size of the cabins as by the obvious feeling of comfort at being at home that was lacking at Mission.

The last day's travel was short but the trails were over river courses and we had to be slow and cautious. Near the river outlet from Stop Lake, not far from where Paul had been narrowly missed by a meteorite that burned through the ice to sizzle then burble in the mud beneath the river, we saw caribou. These were the first we had seen for many miles and there had been few tracks to mar the surface snow along the trail. To my surprise, George did not shoot even though we were only fifteen miles from our destination. He said it was too far to carry the meat with our limited space and tired dogs, but I think it was more likely that he expected to find caribou closer to camp. We finally arrived there about 6:00 P.M. after breaking trail on a long back country detour to avoid the rapids on the river connecting Stop and South Lakes.

1. Over the years I have argued Chipewyan social organization in terms of symbolic factors and kinship. J. G. E. Smith has pursued a different course, arguing from a historical perspective using traditional camping grounds and residence in an ecological context. R. Jarvenpa has used a different set of ecological understandings in his analyses of the Chipewyan farther south in the boreal forest. J. Van Stone and D. M. Smith have focused primarily on village life while T. Irimoto has negated the issue of social organization altogether in his heavily quantified ecological approach. Curiously enough, given the diversity of the approaches utilized, all these works on the Chipewyan manage to complement each other.

2. The version of events given here is one I obtained several times during the period 1969–1975 and is not in accord with information and explanations obtained in 1977 and 1983. By then the Chipewyan as a whole had a better understanding of the operation of bureaucratic processes and understood that communications from the outside required responses from the addressee for action to be taken. When the events occurred, problems of translation, lack of understanding, shyness, and confusion over addresses resulted in a complete breakdown of communication that resulted in the tragedy. There were people in the community, particularly the priest, who normally acted as mediators with the outside world who should have understood what was happening. I have no information on their actions. The Chipewyan are very uncomfortable with

mental illness, relating it to supernatural factors. Avoiding action may have been the most reasonable course of action. In any case, the relevant explanations for the events are not ones based on the private knowledge of the principals but the public explanations shared by the rest of the community. These were the operational factors at the time, which is why they are recounted here.

# Chapter Three

In an area larger than North Carolina, exploited by only a few dozen hunters and their families, that does not contain both the summer and winter ranges of the two greatly diminished caribou herds, it is only the annual caribou migration itself that remains a certainty. Come what may, if there are to be caribou they must each spring go forth upon the barrens to calve and must each winter go into the forest to escape starvation. The locations of the calving areas seem to be almost constant, although an entire herd may have vanished from the northeast Barren Grounds because of the mini ice age (see Smith and Burch 1979; Burch, 1977). Wintering areas change from year to year, but wherever the caribou go in the forest to find food, they must pass twice each year through the northern margin of the transitional forest. The Chipewyan social system exploits this constancy.

In the fall caribou move with the certainty of the elect. No death, accident, or intrusion can long interrupt their search for food or that fabled meadow free of insects. Charged by bears, they flow apart and pass them through; pursued by wolves, they run then watch the dance of death of the unlucky; chased by humans, they sacrifice the chosen and continue on. Until the small lakes freeze and the snow falls they are only passing conscious of concerns other than their own. It is a time when all predators are able to take their fill. A bear may get an occasional cripple. Wolves make virtue of their own laziness and take what they can get: the unwary, the young, the weak, those foolish enough to stand and fight. Humans take their pick.

Before the repeating rifle brought modern firepower into the game late last century, the Chipewyan hunted with muskets, bows, spears, snares, and nets and in coordinated drives on land and water. These methods were as, if not more, effective than modern guns (Townsend

1983). The repeating rifle changed the manner of hunting, allowing men to hunt alone or in twos and threes, so they no longer have to construct fences and corrals or risk their lives in flimsy canoes upon the toss of a bull's antlers.[1] Repeating rifles do not produce more dead caribou than the older methods, but the changes in hunting methods that followed their adoption do produce more waste. Rifles kill by shock effect rather than through hemorrhaging as do blade weapons. Animals that have been shot are frightened by the noise and confusion of their shooting and are often able to run or walk after receiving their wound. Instead of quickly lying down, as is generally the case after penetration by a blade weapon, they may move several miles before stopping. Using a rifle, the hunter can hit caribou at greater distances and in all directions, resulting in a scatter of dead and wounded animals over wide areas. This makes it harder to locate and transport them to the women who process them. The hunter is often unable to butcher the animals at hand before daylight ends, forcing him to abandon pursuit of those wounded animals that have fled. Many escape into the bush to die. Less caribou are killed during the spring migration but even more of the wounded escape to die and feed scavengers and the lesser predators.

In the fall the Chipewyan can take their pick of caribou, and systematically pick and choose they do. Bulls are the sought after prey, bulls with their layer of fat for the rut. That fat is the critical energy source *dene* (the people) need to withstand the winter's cold. Cows are taken only in the absence of bulls or for their hides, their thinner skin producing a more supple leather. Demand for hides is now slight. Calves are taken to make the clothing of small children, their carcasses stored to feed the dogs in the hardest part of the winter.

A choice the Chipewyan still exercise, as they had to exercise it in the past, is to kill far more caribou than appears rational. To be Chipewyan is to kill, eat, and process caribou; to live from the bounty of this species. They say that each spring brings a renewal of the animals and that the number of caribou does not decline from year to year. Chipewyan explain local variations in caribou numbers in terms of their distribution within their total range. If the caribou are not here when they should be, it is because they have gone somewhere else and the relevant issues are "where are they" and "why have they gone." The idea that local absences of caribou are the product of a decline in total numbers is a white man's notion and many *dene* are loath to accept it. Bilingual Chipewyan in particular have difficulty with this issue, having to utilize one set of logic and way of knowing when talking with English speakers and another when speaking and thinking in Chipewyan. Both languages and modes of thought accurately order the observable data, but the Chipewyan mode, assuming that there are caribou in adequate numbers if only one can find where they are, seems more likely to lead to productive action than does the English mode with its implication that there may not be enough caribou no matter what action one takes.

Contemporary Chipewyan speak of the spring migration as an analogue to the fall migration, a source of dry meat to last the summer, but with the passing of year-round bush life its importance has declined. Few families now go north to exploit it. Their declining reliance upon caribou has been offset by exploiting changing patterns of ungulate populations. There have been an astonishing number of forest fires near the village since 1950, with consequent browse production in scrub and second-growth forest. Deer had not been seen near the village for decades when I first went to the field but were breeding there in the early 1980s. By 1975 the moose population was either expanding northward or increasingly migrating in that direction to escape the spring and summer forest fires. The decline in utilization of the spring migration is fortunate, as Chipewyan hunting in the spring is also selective. The preferred animals are still the fattest ones, but the only really fat animals in the spring are the barren cows, yearlings, and healthy pregnant cows.

Chipewyan have very strong ideas about how caribou are to be treated, and respect must be shown for that which is killed. The contemporary diminution of these ideas has not eliminated their concern that killed caribou not be wasted, in and of itself a form of animal abuse that can drive the caribou from a place for years. I have seen resident hunters fail to fully butcher and store caribou only when they were on the trail. Their need for food is immediate and they know they will not return. All other meat is placed into some kind of storage.[2] In the cool days and near freezing nights of late summer, storage may involve no more than stacking and covering the meat. Warmer days require more substantial protection such as burial next to the permafrost or immersion in the ice water of a muskeg. These expedients will keep the meat useable for a considerable time. After the snows begin, meat will last until spring or until it is found by a passing predator.

Meat that is to be dried is brought into camp where it comes under de facto control of the women. That kept as a reserve in the bush is carefully stacked to freeze. More distant meat piles form an extra reserve that draw fox and other scavengers. These are protected by traps that also can yield marketable fur. If there is no other need for the meat, it will feed the dogs. Always, the excess meat is there to meet a crisis. In recent times, the most probable emergencies are losses to animals (especially bear), illness, and the arrival of relatives from places that had no caribou. Frozen meat is useable for months, but it does not have the desirability or vitamin content of fresh meat. The largest single amount of meat is kept in storage in the bush and this may have only a slight probability of being used if caribou remain plentiful. This meat tends to be taken after the men begin to move around with the snow and the condition of the bulls has begun to deteriorate in the rut. Early kills, made when the bulls are in their prime are most likely to be made into dry meat. Dry meat is not subject to taste deterioration over a winter and can last for a year or more but is almost always eaten sooner. Dry meat has qualities other than taste that make it suitable for storage, the most obvious being that storage itself is less of a problem. It takes less space, is less dependent upon temperature for preservation, and can be kept inside the camp. Storing it there reduces its exposure to bear and other bush hazards, but care must be taken so that the dogs do not get loose and get at it.

When meat is consumed in its dried form, more of it can be eaten in a shorter time. This is most desirable during travel when a compressed ration is useful, but it may be important when supplies of dried animal fat or its contemporary substitute, lard, are in short supply. Caribou meat does not marble like American domestic beef. The fat on the animal is located inside the pelvic structure, alongside the intestines and internal organs, and in a layer stretching from midback to the genitals. More care goes into removing fat from the carcass than to any other aspect of the butchering. Since caribou meat is so lean, it is relatively low in calories and should be thought of as a protein source rather than as a calorie source. I have known

Chipewyan to come into the village, even though they had plenty of meat, because it was taken too late in the season to have any fat. They say eating this meat is like eating ice.[3]

The Chipewyan form small residential clusterings of kin and affines to exploit their environment. These clusters are called by reference to the location, activity, person, or persons in the camp. The words that identify the camp are more a description than a name in the English sense of the word (J.G.E. Smith 1981; Helm 1981:297). These clusters are generally restricted, bilateral descent groups with frequently varying composition. They have corporate aspects and can exist intermittently for several generations. In the bush phase of Chipewyan existence each hunting unit must be an autonomous subsistence unit. If not, it cannot establish or maintain a separate existence and it dissipates. These small-scale production units are dispersed throughout the entire northern part of the regional band's total range.[4] Many factors enter into the choice of the specific area a hunting unit occupies in any given season or part of a season, but the dispersal itself is crucial to capitalizing on the caribou migrations. The area each hunting unit can effectively exploit is relatively small, but the collective result of their spacing is a net-like obstacle the caribou must penetrate on their migrations. As long as the caribou pass through the region, at least some of the hunting units will be in position to exploit them. In times when the caribou herds are larger, the systemic pattern of hunting unit dispersal may not be necessary and might vanish. If there are enough caribou, it really doesn't matter where anyone goes.

Before the trading posts led to changes in Chipewyan settlement patterns, the definitions of social groups and their boundaries would have been different and more fluid but the effect would have been the same: the pattern of distribution of the social groups assures enough caribou are killed to keep the population functioning. As the size and distribution of the caribou herds fluctuated, large areas of ground might have to be abandoned for considerable periods in a fallowing process as the Chipewyan moved to seek out where they had gone. Not all the Chipewyan in a regional band have to be formed into hunting units for this effect to be realized. Individuals and indi-

vidual hunting units were free to move deep into the forest or far out
onto the barren grounds as their fancy took them.

Each group now, and probably more so in the past, is able to kill
caribou far in excess of its immediate needs. They do so whenever
they have the opportunity. The survival logic of excess killing should
now be apparent: it is a food reserve that can be distributed to other
Chipewyan. The same pattern of dispersal that ensures that at least
some hunting units will find caribou, greatly increases the probability that others will miss them. The pattern of dispersal of hunting
units and taking surplus meat would have no logic in spite of its effi-
ciency if hunting units were not locked into a system of reciprocity
that ensured that the caribou killed by one group could be passed on
to other groups.

Resources of small game and fish are limited in any area the size a
hunting unit can exploit. These resources are so tied to micro-
environmental variations that few of these limited areas are capable
of supporting a human group the size of a hunting unit over a winter.
If they miss the caribou, these groups must either withdraw to the
village or, when this is not an option, join another group that has
sufficient resources on hand to carry them over until they again
become self-supporting.

The obvious consequence of failing to relocate, at least to outsiders, is starvation, but I was unable to find a fear of starvation or any
realistic stories about it. Starvation is seen as a dramatic end result
of a series of other events such as illness, accident, or travel, rather
than a first cause of death. Its primacy in discussion of the north
owes more to our own history, values, fear of undomesticated land,
and tradition of agricultural famine than it does to any real consideration of life in the north. As far as real starvation, there is a
Chipewyan penchant for using that English word to describe hunger.
When starvation is the topic, English speakers and Chipewyan speaking English are almost always talking about two different things. The
reality of failing to relocate is malnutrition, a condition that can rapidly lead to loss of endurance and illness; serious conditions for members of any small group isolated from the assistance of their fellows.

Simple prudence would seem to dictate going to where food is
rather than going to where it is not. Chipewyan men maintain regular contact with each other and frequently visit other camps. The

people readily detect the presence of others once snow and ice cover the ground and lakes. Their clues can range from tracks to changes in bird flight patterns. Intensely cold atmospheric conditions close to ground level cause boundary layers to form between temperature differences and these seem to act as thermoclines do to sonar, capping the vertical movement of sound waves and producing unexpected effects. Higher pitched sounds, such as dogs howling, can carry for miles whereas sounds of normal volume carry for astonishing distances. It is sometimes possible to recognize voices and hear individual words of normal speech at distances in excess of a mile. The problem of interpreting physical clues is diminished by the knowledge the Chipewyan have of who else should be out there and where they should be. Our unknown "wilderness"⁵ is simply their neighborhood. This network of contact provides for the rapid dissemination of news and gives each man at least a general idea of where the caribou herds are located. If he does not have specific information as to where they are, he has sufficient information to know where to go to find out.

Marcel Mauss (1967), recognizing in B. Malinowski's data the systemic nature of reciprocity that Malinowski himself failed to see, directed anthropology to the unique ability of reciprocity to order and systematize relationships between humans. Since then, most theoretical attention given to reciprocity has been on exchanges that occur in a positive sense: ritual exchanges, feasts, and marriage alliances that involve giving things. Chipewyan men provide an important case in which reciprocity and exchange rarely take this positive form. Chipewyan do give gifts and there are features in their culture that can be seen as public exchanges but most reciprocity operates in a different manner. Although the following description risks distortion through oversimplification, large parts of their system operate through regulating the right to take without asking and the right to refuse a request. This is particularly pronounced in bush life with exchanges of traditional foodstuffs.

In brief, there is a gender-based dichotomy in the practice of reciprocity pivotal to the operation of the traditional Chipewyan system. Women do the work that converts raw game into food and in normal circumstances control the allocation and use of human food within the camp.⁶ This includes preparation of meals and packing the lunches men take into the bush as well as budgeting food supplies. The categories male and female are conceptualized and symbolically treated in such a way that the category male is much more highly valued than the category female. What is true of the relationship between categories at the symbolic level is not totally without reflection in the social practice of gender roles. In spite of this, Chipewyan men responsible for a household rarely will interfere with the women responsible for a household. They can almost always effectively assert the right to do so, making their reluctance all the more conspicuous.

When a household is in need of foodstuffs the woman or women[7] of the household can either go to another household for a visit and, in the course of visiting, request the desired food from the woman or women there or a child can be sent with a request for the food. Chipewyan are quite sociable among themselves and there is frequent visiting from household to household. The more isolated or homogeneous the camp, the more this is true, thus it is not often that women need to make a special visit to obtain food. Sharing between women is part of a continuous stream of socialization and information exchange between residences and results in a constant flow of food. These systematic borrowings tend to involve small amounts suited to the preparation of a meal or to meet a day's needs. Kinship and other factors that determine closeness of relationship affect the nature of the sharing. The closer the relationship between any two women the more likely they are to know each other's immediate needs and the more likely an exchange will be a gift, an unasked for portion, to meet a known need. Knowing of the need in the absence of closeness is less likely to produce a gift, making a request necessary. These exchanges ultimately affect the nature of the relationships between men and are in turn affected by the nature of the men's relationshps and alliances, but they are conducted by the women without any direct reference to the men. Certainly there is no thought of seeking their permission.

Since it is food exchanges between women that make the reciprocity system function, it stands to reason that it is the nature of the relationships between its own women and women of other groups that a hunting unit must take into account during the times it needs to draw upon food resources beyond its own social boundaries. This is no less true because men express their relationship to other groups in terms of their ties to its men rather than to or through women.[8] Men obtain food and women process and distribute it. It is the very mundanity of it, the lack of attention paid to women quietly relating to each other that gives the entire social system the flexibility to distribute food to ensure the survival of everyone.

The existence of bilateral kinship among the Chipewyan and their neighbors is one of the more contentious issues among Northern Athapaskanists. Northern Athapaskan societies, for all their similarities in material culture, form a gradient from northwest to southeast in terms of the complexity of their social organizations as understood by traditional evolutionary models. The direction of the gradient roughly corresponds to the probable direction of the spread of their cultures. There is some linguistic evidence (Dyen and Aberle 1974) that proto-Athapaskan, the presumed mother language of all contemporary Athapaskan tongues, had a matrilineal kinship terminology. These two factors raise the question of why the supposedly more primitive kinship form, matriliny, gave way in the less complex social systems in the east but remained in the more complex social systems in the west.

Almost all of this debate is based upon an archaic typological approach to kinship and social organization (Yerbury 1980, 1986; Bishop and Kretch 1980) that fails to recognize that all societies routinely recognize kinship through both parents (Morgan 1964:430–442) and that take no account of social dynamics or kinship ideology. Kinship operates in so many contexts that it is often not easy to label a society as one of the classic kinship types, or profitable to assume similarity between societies carrying the same label (Needham 1974). Calling the Chipewyan bilateral is a recognition that there are no special rights, obligations, or inequivalent set of kin received through a single parent except those enshrined in Canadian law. Treaty Indian status is passed on differentially in exactly the form found in a patrilineal society. A woman's legitimate child takes the status of her husband, her illegitimate child takes her own status. A man's legitimate child takes his own status, his illegitimate child takes its mother's status.

Chipewyan recognize kinship on three different sets of criteria: birth, marriage, and relative age. Adoption, the logical fourth method, is used, but its practice varies widely within the community and is in a period of rapid change. The first two mechanisms need no explanation but the third may be unfamiliar. The kinship terminology contains terms that may be applied between two people upon the basis of similarity or difference in perceived chronological age. This mechanism is a form of fictive kinship similar to our inclination to apply the terms aunt and uncle to unrelated persons of a senior generation with whom there is some form of sustained interaction or affection. The process is used to create kin ties between people we call grandparents, aunts, uncles, cousins, and grandchildren,[9] but the meaning of the Chipewyan words is not the same as the English words even when both are applied to persons standing in an identical position of biological relatedness.[10]

Chipewyan kinship terminology and usage create a series of categories within which there is no terminological means of differentiation between individuals. A cousin (sela) is a cousin and is formally due the obligations owed a cousin no matter what the nature of the particular individual's specific relationship to the speaker. These series of relationships with the same formal claims on the speaker involve so many people that it is impossible to honor them equally. It is only possible to conform to the appropriate behavior when some nonkinship mechanism temporarily or permanently restricts the number of individuals. There are a number of mechanisms that accomplish this, such as anger, avoidance, or conflict, but the easiest and most used is physical separation. In the village a person may have twenty cousins living within a few hundred yards, but in the bush those same cousins may be scattered over thousands of square miles. Manipulation of this multiplicity of relationships is one aspect of the expression of power in interpersonal relationships and one of the mechanisms that produce the spacing of hunting units in the bush. Within the village a hunting unit cannot maintain its integrity as a subsistence unit because its members have too many conflicting obligations. Physical separation limits and protects its social boundaries so that kin ties may be used to pattern social interaction.

Consideration of Chipewyan kinship and social organization must take account of the strong egalitarian nature of the culture. They have no toleration of hierarchy within a category, and have difficulty with many of the built-in hierarchies of age and gender. They do not assert this as an ideology of equality but through their individual refusal to sanction assertions of superiority by other Chipewyan. It is not an abstract statement of "we are all equal" but a specific refusal to entertain the idea that anyone is "better than I am." This is partly true even in the case of gender. Women accept categorical statements of inferiority and social practices confirming their inferiority, while individually refusing to give moral acceptance. Much of the potential explosiveness of this conflict, which goes beyond gender, is contained through the careful use of context.

The strong egalitarian nature of the Chipewyan conflicts with the logic of a number of kinship categories, and that conflict in the sibling terms is of direct relevance to the situation described here. The terms for siblings are not ones of equality but of hierarchy. There are two terms for brother and two terms for sister, each taking account of the birth order of the sibling relative to that of the speaker. One has not a brother but an elder brother or a younger brother; not a sister but an elder sister or a younger sister. Chipewyan are largely raised by their elder siblings, and once past the toddler stage cease to receive the parental attention they had when younger, unless they happen to be the last-born child. Birth order tends to correspond to physical size and strength through early adolescence. The physical advantages of age are backed by the moral authority of kinship ideology, which holds that the younger should listen to and respect the elder. This seems to work in childhood, but as physical diversification increases among early teens, it begins to run into difficulty as adult gender considerations come increasingly into play. By the time male siblings approach adulthood the built-in authority allocated to the elder brother comes into conflict with the desire of the younger brother to establish his own independence as a social entity. The time when the younger brother breaks free from the role previously played vis-à-vis the elder is dangerous to the integrity of all existing relationships within the social field defined by their close kinship and affinal ties.

Chipewyan never fail to take account of gender differences among adults and this generally carries down into the behavior of children. Relations between sisters are less competitive, or rather, competition is expressed in different ways and occurs in different situa-tions.[11] Marriage tends to restrain competition between sisters by sep-arating them at an early age. Males love their sisters and feel they should respect their older sisters. In practice, however, males tend to ignore any sister as soon as they are large enough and strong enough to defend themselves from her. For males, in this gender conscious society, a sister is but a woman no matter how much she is loved or respected.

The primary categorically ordered source of conflict for existing social groups comes as maturing younger male siblings attempt to assert their autonomy while elder male siblings attempt to sustain their own birth-ordered authoritative superiority. This creates a poten-tially unstable situation in those hunting units with male siblings close together in age. In effect, each hunting unit is oriented toward one adult male. The maturation of the younger males poses a threat to the unit's continuation and his position of influence. As long as he is able to remain active and is reasonably astute, he should be able to use his influence and authority to get younger males to restrain their conflict out of respect for him. He is not able to direct the behav-ior of adult or near adult males, therefore a failure to generate enough respect may result in his replacement as most influential figure or the departure of one or more of the younger men.

The role of affines in Chipewyan culture must be seen in light of this potential for conflict between brothers structured into the inter-action between Chipewyan egalitarianism and their ideas about kin-ship. Chipewyan affinal terminology for the persons called "brother-in-law" and "sister-in-law" in English lacks the feature of age grading that is part of the sibling terminology. Without the birth-order dis-tinction, these terms lack the idea of an ordered distribution of author-ity within ego's generation. Birth-ordered hierarchy is also absent in the cousin terminology. These terms, however, can be applied on the basis of relative age within the community. Outside the community speakers apply the cousin term to mean "someone from the same community as myself." Women frequently use the "cousin by rela-tive age" as a form of address to female age mates, but the terms pri-marily refer to ties created by descent. The children of siblings are cousins and the children of cousins are cousins, both the product of existing relationships in the previous generation. Siblings-in- law are the product of a new relationship created by marriage and have a characteristic that results in an orientation toward them rather than cousins in the formation of intergroup alliances. Siblings-in-law come to exist simultaneously in both ego's generation and ego's parent's generation. Ego's parents acquire ego's spouse's parents as a set of siblings-in-law identical in form and terminology[12] to the set of siblings-in-law ego acquires.

The formation of hunting units is affected, indeed only definable, by *inkoze. Inkoze* specifically refers to sorcery and death by sorcery, but I use the term as a metonym for an entire complex of ideas and practices. It is knowledge about the operation of the universe revealed to humans by supernatural creatures in dreams. From the time of Hearne in the 1770s to present day anthropological works, writers on the Chipewyan have found it necessary to make reference to *inkoze* to explain the Chipewyan way of life, even when their interest is in other aspects of *dene* life. The best sources on the subject are David M. Smith's (1973, 1982) two monographs, which are rich in the ethnographic detail of *inkoze* in routine life and provide an invaluable picture of it as sorcery.

Our culture and language create a distinction between the natural and the supernatural as modes of explanation, but as Levy-Bruhl (1967, 1979) pointed out in the early part of this century, to accept this distinction is a cultural decision that presupposes explanation in natural terms as the only true explanation. Supernatural explanation is relegated to other realms of a lesser reality. The Chipewyan do not make this distinction between the natural and the supernatural as modes of explanation. Where their practice approximates our own, they make the distinction in different ways. The English speaker must come to see as a unity what our language and culture insist are separate and opposed entities. *Inkoze* is not just knowledge, it is also power. In a broad sense, it is knowledge of how the world works, and one aspect of knowledge is the ability to achieve particular results. It becomes a complete theory of explanation for the causality of certain kinds of events and for the relationship between those events and particular persons.

In stories and myths the Chipewyan have about their past, *inkoze* was a human property unrestricted by gender. Sometime between the past, as represented in current accounts, and the present, *inkoze* became something only males can have. As the Chipewyan adapted to and created the changes occurring in their lives it is only reasonable to suppose that their ideological systems also changed. The current restriction on the possession of *inkoze* is consonant with other aspects of their life. It is probable that the teachings of the Roman Catholic Church are heavily reflected in the current division of *inkoze* by gender, but the church has not had a uniform affect upon all Chipewyan.[13] Whatever the origin of current practices, they are intertwined with the division of labor and the role caribou play and have played in Chipewyan life.

In the picture that emerges from the myths I have been told, there was a time when human, animal, and supernatural creatures were not discrete entities. What they were is intelligible only in terms of what they became. The Chipewyan say that it was not until the Roman Catholic priests came that a distinctly human Chipewyan language appeared to replace the common tongue of humans and animals, further separating them from *inkoze* and the animals. Once, everyone had *inkoze* and used it even for mundane tasks like making arrowheads or getting water. Now it is rapidly withdrawing from the Chipewyan. Some creatures of *inkoze* still reveal knowledge to men but this happens less and less in each generation. The elderly often choose now to take to their graves what knowledge they are permitted to teach. Europeans have a charter in Chipewyan myth as the controllers of things, control illicitly won in the origins of human diversity. With their ascendancy, their mechanical universe is seen to displace *inkoze* in the affairs of men.

*Inkoze* should not be spoken about. It should not be sought and may not be claimed. To speak openly about it, to claim its possession, is to announce oneself a fraud. Sociologically it is a characteristic achieved by certain men as a result of a wide-reaching consensual process accomplished largely through the gossip of women. Women, divorced from its possession, are the only category of people able to speak freely of it among themselves. All men are potential claimants to *inkoze* but only some have it and fewer have very much of it.

It is at the systemic level that *inkoze* is most easily seen to be a theory of causality and explanation. It is the cause of certain types of events as well as the explanation of why they occur to particular people: a perfect but nonetheless functional tautology. A man is a successful hunter because he has *inkoze*. It is his *inkoze* that causes him to be successful at hunting and that success reveals to others that he has it. Consistent failure would show that he did not have *inkoze* for a man without *inkoze* could not be a successful hunter. The logical effect of *inkoze* as a system of explanation, subtly but imperfectly translated into social reality, is to set all men into a competitive quest for it. The quest is not to claim power but to display the characteristics that reveal that one has power. All relationships between men are, or have the potential to be, competitive.

The competitive nature of *inkoze*, like Chipewyan ideas of egalitarianism, is counter to many aspects of their ideas about kinship relationships. These stress the noncompetitive nature of the relationships, hence all men are competitors, but some categories of kinsmen are potential noncompetitors. It is this aspect of kinship that allows the creation of hunting units and the determination of their boundaries. Sharing is an act largely conducted by women without reference to their men's *inkoze*. Within a hunting unit the sharing between women makes no statement about the relative status of the *inkoze* of the men to whom they are attached. Sharing between hunting units does make a statement, however indirect, about the relationships of *inkoze* between the men attached to the women. The recipient male's group is the weaker of the two in that he has failed to provide what was needed. The boundaries of the hunting unit are precisely at that point where the women are unable to share food without a social statement being made about the supernatural status of their men vis-à-vis each other.

The immediate corollary of this role of sharing and *inkoze* in interhunting unit relations is that in the bush phase of their life the nature of the boundaries of social groups need not be the same for men and women. Men are caught in an implicit web of *inkoze* that governs their interaction with the environment and each other, a web that kinship and proximity can suppress only at the cost of constant effort. Women are outside this web in their relationships with each other and only distantly perceive it as a constant, if implicit,

factor in the relationships of men. There are areas where both genders share concerns of *inkoze* and are familiar with its working but
the thought systems by which the day to day actions of men and
women are perceived are sufficiently different that there is ample
room for misunderstanding of the opposite gender.

1. A favored technique for hunting caribou was to drive a canoe over the shoulders
of a swimming bull. The animal would continue to swim among the herd, pulling the
canoe without scattering the remaining animals. The hunters would stab the
swimming animals in the kidneys with short spears. The technique was productive
but very dangerous, as the towing bull could upset the canoe at the toss of his head.

2. In the two dichotomy system Woodburn (1982:431–434) has proposed, the
Chipewyan are a delayed return system with an egalitarian social system. That they
do not fit his proposed model is perhaps inevitable in an environment where food
storage can be purely a byproduct of climate for three-quarters of the year.

3. This is a curious analogy that may have some relevance to the general mythol-
ogy of cannibal monsters throughout the subarctic.

4. Exploitation of southern areas is based on moose and other resources and is
somewhat different.

5. I have come to have increasing difficulty with our use of this term to designate
an area where there has been an absence of human action on the environment. I have
never quite figured out how I would explain to Mike, heir to sixty or more generations
of *dene*, what "wilderness" meant and that he lived in one.

6. Men control the feeding of the dogs; something not without symbolic significance in this system.

7. The equivocation over the singular-plural is to avoid the issue of status between
women in households that contain more than one woman. That issue is beyond the
scope of this work.

8. The picture presented here is simplified. Reality is complicated by such things
as values about hospitality and ideas of responsibility for failure to help (Slobodin
1960, 1969).

9. Chipewyan kinship terminology and practice vary widely. Part of the reason
May was unsure if all of her siblings survived (Chapter 2) was because in the area of
her birth certain cousins are called siblings. This is not the practice among the people
where she now lives. No systematic comparison of Chipewyan kinship terminology
has yet been published.

10. The cognatic Chipewyan are an exception to the patterns of usage of genealogical position and relative age as structuring principles that Needham (1966) has advanced
from his study of lineal systems.

11. Perhaps the arena for competition between Chipewyan females is so different
from that which I am used to as an alien male observer, that it seems like an entirely
different process to me.

12. The Chipewyan do not work with systematic regulations regarding the application of kinship terminology, and this multitude of nonage graded relationships may
be extended to include spouse's siblings' spouses. I am not aware of extension of the
sibling-in-law terminology in the parents' generation beyond the two actual sets of
parents, but would not be surprised if it did happen when other factors made it reasonable.

13. D. M. Smith (1982) emphatically states that there were always some women with *inkoze* at Fort Resolution. J. G. E. Smith (personal communications n.d.) has repeatedly found reference to current female figures with *inkoze* in communities to the east. My group stoutly denies the idea.

# Chapter Four

Our arrival at the South Lake camp was a relief to the people there, as they had begun to worry about us. May was inclined to worry whenever any of her children were up to something new, and our trip was definitely in that category. She wasn't really worried about George, he routinely made trips like this, but his shepherding me was a horse of a different color.

When we were about five miles out George and I left the trail along the river and cut inland through a series of muskegs to an esker. Being inland felt strange after all those miles of travel along the lakes. George had to pick his way through the unfamiliar terrain while breaking trail because there were no trails in the woods. The day was warm and the snow was wet. Wet snow increases to the load on the dogs, and someone has to travel in front to pack down a path. Ice balls formed and clung to rough surfaces on the toboggan, increasing the drag so much we had to stop every so often and clean them off. This time of year many men put runners on their toboggans to raise the bottom surface and decrease the buildup but we did not have any with us. The dogs suffer from the wet snow, as it packs between their toes, forming large lumps that hurt to walk on and if not promptly removed, soon wear the dogs' pads to bloody stumps. What snow and friction do not do, the dogs accomplish themselves, as they chew at their feet to remove the lumps. The classic solution is to make them small leather moccasins.

The winter camp was built on a small lake, really a long pond, running east off of South Lake. The south shore was a peat deposit and the north shore was a mixture of peat bog and muskeg. The cabins were thirty yards inland on solid ground at the base of the esker. This was an unusual location for a Chipewyan camp and it was generally felt Wellington had erred in choosing it. The rise of the esker and its tree cover gave protection from the wind in all directions, hence it was extremely secluded and felt secure, but there was no view from the camp. The location was only habitable after the muskeg had frozen, as there was no way to get from the cabins to the small lake without getting wet. The muskeg was a haven for the mosquitoes that were already putting in an appearance on the warmer days. The small lake itself was connected to South Lake by a passage no more than five feet wide. This lay between two precipitous rises and was the first place to thaw. To get out on the main ice we either had to cope with the last, hanging shreds of ice and risk getting dunked or make an annoying detour.

George and I got up on the side of the esker and followed it toward camp. We heard it long before we reached it; its sheltered location hid even the smoke from us. The first visual signs of human activity were tree stumps and disrupted deadfall where firewood had been cut. The snow was still deep when Paul, May, and the others had arrived, and they had made paths to the top of the esker to search for wood. The esker's top surface was exposed to the sun, and by the time George and I arrived, most of the snow there had melted.[1] The dogs soon heard us approach and the fuss they made brought the people out to meet us.

The camp consisted of four cabins along a central path (the path came after the cabins) separated by as much as fifty feet. Paul had built a large cabin at the east end and had given it to my wife and me to use. I left the snowmobile near the storage platforms, called stages, close to the stakes for Paul's dog beds. I was immediately struck by the skinned, weather-bleached carcasses of fox and other animals that had been trapped during the fall hanging from the stages. The Chipewyan are reluctant to take the remains of these animals into the bush to dispose of them, yet they must be kept away from the dogs. Paul's explanation for hanging the animals was that their teeth were capable of penetrating the stomach or intestinal walls of any dog that consumes them. Since Chipewyan dogs consume fish as the staple element of their diet and crack and eat animal bones without any Chipewyan worrying about the diet being hazardous, it is safe to say that symbolic concerns were the major reason. My asking was one of those situations where I knew the answer and should not have asked the question, but wanted to hear it said. Having been asked an

impolitic question, Paul politely gave me a plausible answer that did
not touch upon the symbolic aspects that should not be talked about
casually. Hanging their carcasses to keep the dogs from eating them
is a mark of respect for the trapped animals and fits well with the
Chipewyan's declared past practice of preventing dogs from eating
caribou bones.

The next cabin was George's, and it was smaller than his father's.
Both sat on the north side of the trail less than twenty feet apart.
George's dog beds were in the muskeg in front of his cabin and he
put the dogs there soon after our arrival. His cabin lacked the elabo-
rate stages and other subsidiary constructions of his father's cabin. A
hole beside the cabin was the source of sand used to insulate the
roof. Sand is the final layer of insulation, and these sand pits take on
a characteristic shape — the opening narrower than the inside of the
pit. The insulating is done as the ground is beginning to freeze in the
fall, and the sand below the surface is softer and warmer. It is easier
to get it out by making a small opening and hollowing the ground
out underneath. The hole was now being used as a trash pit.

The third cabin was Wellington's, fifty feet from George's and close
to the muskeg on the south side of the trail. His dog beds were in the
muskeg and his stages less complex than Paul's but more so than
George's. Wellington's stages reflected his longer occupancy and contained a good deal of equipment and material hauled in from the outside. The first one to be built, it was a curious cabin. All of the others
faced different directions and were higher up the esker, having a less
enduring but lighter and more spacious feel about them.

The last cabin belonged to Wellington's wife's mother, and was
hurriedly built for her late in the fall of 1974, when she had decided
to spend the season here rather than at the bush village on Missionary Lake. By far the smallest of the lot, only a rough partial floor had
been put into it. Paul and May had taken this cabin for themselves. I
was not there when this decision had been made but it was typical of
them to take the least desirable for themselves. The cabin had two
structures built behind it on the northeast side. One was a tipi used
as a portable smoke tent whose canvas had seen service for many
years in many camps. The canvas was on its last legs but would survive use at yet two more camps. The other structure was a tipi-shaped
outhouse with a truncated top that was constructed from spruce

cuttings. This was the only tipi-shaped structure I ever saw in the bush that was not a smoke tent. I thought at first it might be a menstrual seclusion hut built for little Ann, Paul and May's granddaughter, but seclusion practices for girls reaching menarche were a thing of the past.

Wellington had been camping on this lake for several years, while the rest of his family were farther north or east. This coalescence of kin and affines around Wellington had begun to develop after 1970 as he established his own autonomy by moving away from his parents. Before 1974–1975, the fall clustering had always formed around Paul and May. This second instance of residing with Wellington helped set the stage for his potential advancement to most influential man in the group.

Resident in camp were myself, my wife, and our two children, one four years and one eight months; George and Joan and their two children, a girl two-and-a-half and an infant boy; Wellington and Ann with two boys, nine and five, and an infant girl. Paul and May had with them their grandchildren, little Ann, Mickey, and Mike.

All three of the children with Paul and May were grandchildren by genealogical position, children of their own children. Mike was the second son of Wellington and Ann and was being raised by his grandparents as a son. He applied parental kinship terminology toward them and was addressed by other people in the camp mostly by name. When pressed for a kin term designation for him, Wellington's younger siblings professed some uncertainty and decided him to be a "brother," using the English term rather than the Chipewyan one. I did not push Wellington on the point but I never heard him call Mike by anything other than his name. I have heard him refer to Mike as "my son."

The Chipewyan kinship terminology is one of both address and reference, but its use as a system of address is rapidly fading. In the situation here it is easy to see how the use of names can bypass difficult classifications and let people avoid sensitive situations. Each Chipewyan has a family name, required and sometimes assigned by the Canadian government. Some of these names are attempts either at the translation of a Chipewyan name or to create Chipewyan-sounding English words. Names are given, and now recorded, in church records in English. Each English name has a Chipewyan pronunciation and sometimes the recognized Chipewyan equivalent of an English name is an entirely different word. In addition to family names and first names, people generally have a Chipewyan nickname and it is by this name that they are known among themselves. Chipewyan have a propensity to change their names if they become dissatisfied with them or the circumstances surrounding their use. This does make collecting names a bit of a problem, as few people know all the variants for persons not close to them. To return to the issue of Mike's kin–name usage; what made it unusual was his dogged insistence that Paul and May were his parents and that Wellington and Ann were not. He was, at his young age, taking an active part in defining both his personal history and identity as well as the social environment in which he lived.

The presence of little Ann and Mickey was connected through the common circumstance of the loss of a parent to disease. Mickey's mother died of meningitis while her marriage was still in its early years. First-born, he was placed in a foster home in Parklund (Dyck 1980) after she died. A few years later his father (Fred, Paul and May's eldest son) left bush life to work at the mine, in large part to be able to afford to visit his children regularly. He was able to keep in touch, visiting them in Parklund in spite of the considerable expense. Mickey's sister was happy in Parklund and remained there, but Mickey had gone to Mission for a visit the previous summer and refused to leave his father. He had forgotten how to speak Chipewyan and was in the throes of relearning it, so this first lengthy venture into the bush was a formidable experience for him.

In the village, Fred had lived next to Paul and May with his wife. Paul wanted to burn the dwelling where his son's wife had died, but was talked out of it so that the dwelling could be taken over by Virginia, his newly married daughter. Her husband later contracted meningitis and was taken to the hospital in Minetown, one hundred miles west of Mission. Upon arrival he was immediately sent on to the provincial university hospital but he died en route. The people of the village were advised of his death and they raised the money to have the body shipped home. Neither the money nor the body were returned. Virginia had married young and was but nineteen when her husband died. She was unable to accept that he was dead and became disfunctional. In her denial of his death and in her grief, she came to blame herself for it. During her period of grief, responsibility for her two daughters, Barb and little Ann, fell upon May. After Virginia recovered and later remarried, the relationship between May and the two girls remained strong.

Paul again wanted to burn the house but Wellington took it over and was still using it as his village residence.

### Paul

Paul was the youngest of three sisters and two brothers surviving to adulthood. He was born on the north shore of Stop Lake in 1918 and it is here he thinks of as home. In common with his generation, he grew up in the bush. His first trip to the store came at eleven, an experience he vividly remembers. On top of an esker, near this place where he was born, lie the graves of two of his and May's infant children, who died shortly after birth in the 1940s.

In 1975 two of his sisters and his father still lived, the old man in his nineties. Blind and hard of hearing, he lived in a neighboring settlement with one of his daughters. Paul rarely visited them even though they were but a dozen miles away, and, in turn, was little visited by them. His brother died young and the death affected Paul deeply. He still makes veiled allusions to him when death takes a personal reference. This may be related to Paul's intense interest in *inkoze*. As a young man he was building a reputation as a healer and was frequently visited by his power source, but because of May's fear of the creature's visits, the relationship cooled after his marriage.

Paul stands between five feet seven and five feet nine inches, and is of medium build with average strength and endurance for a Chipewyan. He was noted for his skill as a hunter and near virtuosity with a .22, a weapon that still delights him. He is the only man in the region I know with the reputation for effectively hunting caribou with that weapon, routinely killing even running caribou by shooting them in the kidneys. He had more than a passing fancy for the demon rum in his youth and is still teased about the empty beer bottles he packed nearly two hundred miles so his home brew did not have to be drunk from a cup. In accordance with Chipewyan conventions of drinking, Paul regulated his alcohol consumption by controlling the situations in which he would drink rather than avoiding excess when he did drink. He seems never to have had a drinking problem but one purpose his drinking sometimes served was to allow the expression of hostilities normally kept hidden.

In his late fifties, Paul presents a somewhat deceptive image of a mellow man of even disposition and little passion. Anger does not come easily now and control quickly returns when it does. He has largely put aside whatever dreams and ambitions he had as a young man and his life is increasingly focused upon his immediate family. Never a man prone to express affection, he astounded his family when he began to dote on Mike and his other grandchildren.

With a heavy emotional commitment to bush life as a hunter and trapper, he is striving almost with desperation to maintain his independence. He was not greatly slowed by his heart attack in 1972, but his emphysema is exacting a progressively greater toll. In 1975, his ability to perform the more strenuous activities bush life demands of a man was increasingly restricted and he sometimes had problems with routine tasks. My conversations with others indicate that he has turned more toward philosophical aspects of Chipewyan culture and lives in fear of twin evils: helplessness and dying in the village. Aside from simply liking him, I found the most compelling aspect of the man, was his streak of bloody-minded empiricism about things others approach in an irrational manner. In a sequence of divinations made in the late spring and in the fall, he systematically experimented, using different kinds of scapulae, different means of marking, and different means of scorching. Paul alone among all the men saved the scapulae to see which had worked best under each set of circumstances.

My overriding memory of him comes from my first trip into the Northwest Territories in 1970 when we were camped on the north shore of Foxholm Lake. As it darkened, the camp was quiet with the satisfaction of a productive day well completed when suddenly all the dogs rose and faced south into a mild breeze blowing from the opposite shore. They commenced to howl and bark even as their hackles rose. My own dog stayed close by the tents and displayed the same behavior, although he was free to move about and leave camp if he chose. We were only a few dozen feet from the lake shore and it was more than a mile to the other side. We hoped the dogs had smelled wolves, a sign that the caribou had returned. The camp froze as all the adults and older children came outside to see what was causing the disturbance. The women stood and talked quietly among themselves in front of the listening smaller children while the men searched south of the camp then moved east to the crest of a small ridge a few hundred feet away. We searched the ridge from a quickly formed skirmish line. By the time we reached the downslope to the lakeshore we had excluded the possibility of bear or small animals near the camp as the cause of the dogs' excitement and had assured ourselves that nothing of a supernatural nature was in the vicinity of camp. We talked together on the hillside for a few minutes and discussed the possibilities. We were unable to explain what was scaring the dogs, so everyone started back to the tents. It was by now as dark as it ever gets in such clear air under cloudless skies, but here Paul stopped. Waving the rest of us on he returned to the crest of the ridge where he sat on a large rock facing into the wind across the lake. I went in and out of my tent for nearly an hour, watching him waiting and listening. I realize that my feelings, drawing upon every romantic stereotype of Indians, the north, and wilderness I had ever experienced, had little to do with his feelings and thoughts, but it was a curiously intense sharing of context rather than meaning that left me never more understanding of this man or more alien from him.

The people at South Lake had pragmatic reasons for being glad to see us whatever their emotional concerns. Since their arrival it had been cold, turning warm enough to melt the snow only just in time for George and I to have difficulty on our last day's travel. All the dry wood close by had been used in previous occupations and it had been hard for them to get out and get firewood. I had Paul's toboggan, so he was not able to use his dogs to haul in wood. Drinking water had also been a problem. The small off-shoot bay of South Lake was shallow and had frozen nearly to the bottom. The water hole had to be dug through six or more feet of ice and the water underneath was yellowish-brown muskeg water. It was potable but did not suit their aesthetics. In the abundance of clear, clean, and superbly palatable water in this vast emptiness, the Chipewyan can be downright picky about water quality, taste, and temperature.

The thing that had disturbed them most before we arrived was a red fox found dead on the doorstep of the cabin Paul and May were to use. Inexplicably dead animals are not common here and Paul feared this fox was a portent of something unfortunate to come or having already happened elsewhere to someone in the family. His fears did not help raise the pall cast by the cold, deep snow, poor water, and feeling of isolation. To make matters worse, there had been no sign of the caribou that were the rationale for our being here this early in the season. When George and I arrived we were able to confirm that the caribou were not east or north of South Lake, so there was no need to fear we had already missed them. Optimism increased when Wellington arrived in camp on April 24. His departure had been delayed and he had taken a shorter and more difficult route, making up much of the time lost to the late start. He had come inland after passing Navy Lake, the way caribou would come, and had killed seven of them at the south end of the lake. He was too heavily laden to bring them on into camp so the carcasses were left there, skinned, butchered, and stacked on the lake ice. The certainty of caribou yet to come complemented the few pieces of fresh meat he had brought along and soon the talk was of making enough dry meat to last the entire summer. Wellington told me he wanted fifty caribou for dry meat. On Friday, George killed three on the ice of the main lake not far from camp.[2]

The weather turned warm and sunny with concomitant melting and deterioration of the trail system, and travel was largely restricted to the lake itself. Crossing the narrows between the small lake and the large one became increasingly hazardous. I thought it was for this reason that Wellington was hesitant to go out and recover the meat of the seven caribou he had stacked on the lake. George quickly got out and brought in the meat of the three animals he had killed. It was the distribution of the meat of these animals and the need to use dry meat supplies from the past winter that alerted me to the trouble brewing in camp.

Apparently none of the meat from George's caribou made its way to Wellington's house. Fresh meat had made it to my place and to Paul and May's house, and I didn't think to ask if Wellington had any. With his own caribou still in the bush and the small quantity he had brought with him distributed and eaten, he had on hand no meat of his own. This is exactly the kind of situation the women's normal visiting and sharing solves quickly and smoothly. My first indication of trouble came when I was told May was grousing about Joan, not to her but in her house, in the presence of other women and children, saying that she had not sent meat to Ann. It was dry meat rather than fresh meat that was the topic of discussion. Joan quickly had little Ann take some to Ann's house. If things had been working as they should, there would have been no need for May to intervene. Joan knew full well that Wellington and Ann did not have the meat they needed. It is only outsider males who do not know such things as who has what to eat, how much they have of it, and how long they have had it.

I had expected difficulty between George and Wellington on the basis of my past experience with them, their structural positions and points in their life cycles, and the comments I had gotten from Paul and May in Vancouver. I had not expected the difficulty to have reached the point of showing up among the women at this early stage of my visit. If I had not been following these people's lives over the last five years it would have looked like the trouble began among the women and then spread to the men rather than the other way around.

Many of the supplies stored in the bush cannot be replaced except at a store and all are an integral part of the life-support system. Things that may have little intrinsic value have value added to them because of the distance from the stores and the cost in time, effort, and money to get them. No one is expected to be in need while supplies sit unused, but it is poor form for a borrower to allow the owner to go into the bush expecting to find the supplies and then have to undergo deprivation because the owner was not told that the supplies had been used. The ideas and practices attached to caches in the north are strong and violation of them can lead to violence. When I began to investigate this situation, a series of stories about George's wife Joan, began to surface. George never did hear most of the stories unless Joan herself decided to tell him.

One such incident had occurred the previous fall. As the fall season drew to a close, the families began to leave the bush camp for the Christmas season in the village. Wellington had departed before his parents and George. After he had gone, possibly after Paul and May had left, George went off into the bush for some reason or other. In his absence Joan went into Wellington's dwelling and helped herself to some of the supplies. Little Ann had seen her enter the house and take the supplies. During Christmas Joan did not tell anyone what she had done. Wellington and Ann arrived this spring to find the now irreplaceable supplies missing. To make matters worse, Joan had not been out of those items and had no need for them. Little Ann told no one what she had seen until the supplies were found to be missing on our return to the camp, a lack of judgment prompted by a child's sense of discretion. This incident added to the negative view of Joan

widely held in the camp. Not all the approbation stopped with Joan.
As Joan's husband, George's reputation was intimately tied to hers
and he had a responsibility to keep his wife under control. How he
was supposed to know she did these things if no one would tell him
is not entirely clear to me, but it does demonstrate that any person's
position (status, reputation) is not an independent entity but is linked
to the actions of persons connected to them.

The first rain of the season came on April 29. It did little to cheer
anyone up, but it was followed by cold weather which did, having
the twin advantages of preserving some of the more crucial sections
of the trails and killing off the first of the mosquitoes.[3] This part of
April wasn't very busy. The caribou migration was moving up the
frozen lakes, and it took little effort to tell if they were in our area.
My notes for this period show us making trips to different parts of
the lake and the back places not often gotten to in the deep of winter, always alert to caribou but mostly just exploring. The routes of
travel and the terrain are so sensitive to the weather that knowing
an area in one season may not be much help in other seasons.

My time in camp was productive as my companions spent a good
deal of time talking about past life and magical power, a subject
Wellington did not speak of too much. Just what that dead red fox
Paul found on his doorstep meant came up several times but no consensus emerged. George seemed partial to the idea that a hurt and
now vanished dog he had left behind at Christmas had killed it, and
he hoped it meant the dog would return. Paul feared it might indicate trouble among family elsewhere: a sign of events of an unpleasant nature. To all intents and purposes, Wellington simply did not
care about the dead fox. I have no indication that the women expressed
a guess as to its meaning, but they did repeat the men's guesses. They
seemed less disturbed by the fox being dead on the doorstep than
they were by the fact that the men were worried. Obviously, I was
not privy to their discussions among themselves, and I may be mis-
reading the nature and extent of their concern. In one sense the fox
had become a symbol of the difficulties in the relationships within
the camp. Paul worried the topic like a teething puppy worries an
old slipper, hanging on to it long after everyone else had lost interest.
His linking the possible portent of the fox to the rest of his kin back
in the village was a way to assert the identity of the larger group

from which this camp was drawn. The assertion that the actions of people here had consequences for the wider kin set was a way to emphasize the unity of the group. His worries were a plea not to let the conflict here get out of hand.

On April 30, caribou still not in evidence, Wellington, George, and I made a trip north to where the river leaves South Lake for Stop Lake. These two lakes are links in a major drainage system flowing into Hudson Bay. So much of this country is lake that rivers are but a disjointed series of connections between them. At these connecting points the water makes adjustments for changes in elevation with short bursts before falling into the steadiness of a major lake, the motion concentrated at rapids rather than along the whole length of the rivers. In some places the water is so rapid in its flow that it does not freeze all winter. What ice does form at these places is often thin, easy to break through from either top or bottom, and may break up at any time. The energy expended here is crucial to the survival of many species of mammals and birds, as the open water is a source of food for air-breathing fish eaters, like the otter, as well as a last refuge for fish-eating ducks whose young are not mature enough to migrate until late fall. In spring these open places are concentration points for migrating waterfowl. Mallards and Canada geese arrive in March or early April when everything else is snow covered and frozen.

On this trip I first saw what was to become characteristic of the hunting relations between George and Wellington. After we had been at the river a short while we saw an otter swimming. We were on the south shore about a hundred feet from the open place, and the otter had a stretch of only a few hundred yards long in which to swim without going under the ice. Otter is one of the more valuable furs in the trapper's panoply of pelts and even in late spring it is valuable in spite of the deterioration of a winter's wear and tear on the hair. We spent some time in pursuit of the otter, moving back and forth along the wooodline, but only Wellington shot at it. Our pursuit was not really serious as we knew full well that killing the otter would result in its being swept down river under the ice, destroying the value of the pelt if we were lucky enough to recover it.

Any time you have three armed men and one target, a moving one at that, there is an inherent competitiveness in the situation. Under other circumstances[4] George and Wellington's degree of relatedness would have allowed us to shoot at the otter without the distinction as to who actually hit it having any particular significance. I really don't remember how I sensed that I should not shoot, but I probably took a lead from George and did not shoot because he did not. George is generally a more sensitive person than Wellington and prefers to follow the rules and conventions of courtesy. Wellington, more aggressive and less interested in convention, just barged ahead and shot. George's not shooting was a recognition of his brother's claim to the otter and the right to its pelt if it had been killed. What should have been a friendly exercise of marksmanship whose significance was joint participation became instead a statement of distinctness.

As early as April 28, George had expressed some of his concerns about the possibility of Wellington getting the fish camp. He was decidedly ambivalent about the situation, but mostly his attention was on caribou hunting and the past trapping season, the fish camp itself remaining of interest mostly to Wellington. It was now the tail end of April and it looked like we might not catch much of the migration at all. The problem of locating the tents for the summer camp was being discussed as the women worked to get the tents ready. There was hope that wind and rain might drive the melt water off the lake surface so the caribou would follow the large frozen lakes instead of trails deep in the woods. There was a reluctance to face the possibility of having to move before the caribou kills necessary for the dry meat had been made. May was the only one in camp with the skill to make a tent from scratch and she was busily sewing one together for one of her sons. This itself is an indication of how skill at some task may be seen as a basis of power and how the complementarity of the sexual division of labor creates power by dividing tasks so that dependence is created even where there is nothing in the task itself that would limit it to being performed by a single gender.

While George, Wellington, and I were down at the river on April 30, Paul took Mike out on the lake to hunt for caribou. They saw caribou but were unable to kill any because Mike scared them away. Paul's eyesight was fading, leaving him farsighted. He had difficulty focusing on the target and seeing the sights of his rifle, hence his marksmanship was dropping off. The few caribou we had seen had been scattered and we had had little luck killing any. The sighting of these caribou and May's near completion of the tent prompted action on relocation to the tents. On May 1st, George, Wellington, and I went over the lake to inspect the site where the tents were to be set.

Among the multitude of large and spectacular lakes in this area, South Lake is thoroughly unremarkable. It is more or less circular, really more teardrop in shape. The river enters in the south and flows out to the north. The main lake is only about ten miles from top to bottom and four to six miles wide. The lake is studded with islands of sand and gravel with several larger ones that are part of a single esker. The country around the lake tends to be rocky rather than the open parkland that makes far such easy walking. Our winter camp on the offshoot bay/lake was on the eastern shore where the lake begins to narrow into the stretched part of the teardrop. The location chosen for the summer camp was along the western shore of the teardrop where a long projecting esker points south into the lake, facing in the direction caribou were expected to come. The esker rises thirty to fifty feet above the lake surface and gives unhindered visibility for some miles to the south before a large sand island blocks the view. The fly-in fish camp was located on the western end of this east–west oriented island. The views to the west and east are largely unhindered by the terrain, but tree growth on the esker interfered with the view west. This was not thought important, as the trees provided wood and neither the caribou nor anything else were expected to come from that direction.

Wellington had used this esker as a summer camp several times. It was high and dry with a good exposure to the wind to help blow away the black flies and mosquitoes. It was only a mile-and-a-half to two miles, depending on the route, from the winter camp. We loaded onto the snowmobile and toboggan. Wellington drove while George steered the toboggan from a standing position at its rear. I ended up a passenger, about the only activity in which you first get frostbitten on your rear. Three-quarters of the way across the the lake we saw caribou. Wellington launched us in a pursuit that took us over several miles of the lake to the western shore near the fish camp. As we got closer we could see there were eleven in the bunch, a mixture of cows and yearlings.

These caribou either had not been hunted by snowmobile before or had not learned their lesson. Experienced animals run as soon as they see a snowmobile, the wisest run into the closest brush they can find and keep on going. These animals did not run until they had stood and watched the snowmobile approach and then ran only a short way into the brush. Wellington drove the snowmobile and tobog- gan headlong into the brush at the lake shore, and both he and George leapt from the vehicles, and tore after the caribou at a dead run. By the time I managed to disentangle myself from the inside of the tobog- gan and get through the deep snow and willow brush, they were out of sight. I tried to take a short cut and learned why they had chosen to run over the only well-timbered surface around: their route had no underbrush to entangle them and the firm sand surface supported a much shallower snow cover than did more sheltered areas. Wellington is taller and stronger than George and was able to run through the snow faster than his brother. He shot four of the cari- bou. George did not shoot even though he came in sight of the cari- bou and could have killed some. The situation called for immediate action but also for a display of judgment in a measured response. The caribou fled into the bush but had not kept on going. Too precip- itous a response might have succeeded only in frightening them, caus- ing them to run farther into the bush and out of range. The same dynamics as those at the river were at work again. Wellington first saw the caribou, as he had first seen the otter, and was the first to shoot, while George chose not to shoot at all. Wellington took all the game that had been killed as he would have taken the otter if it had been killed.

I must qualify the last statement about taking of all of the game. The conventions for fur-bearers are a bit different from those for food animals. When the Chipewyan hunt food animals together, the kill is divided among all of the hunters. A man hunting unsuccessfully with another man, even though separated from his successful hunt- ing companion, will claim to have killed what his partner has killed and is entitled to half of the kill. Butchering an animal that has been killed can be seen as a claim to the animal being butchered. It is cus- tomary, when someone has killed a number of animals or a very large animal like a moose, for passers-by or other people there to help butcher, but they make sure it is known that their help is not a claim to what they butcher. These conventions work more firmly when the people involved are not close kin or part of the same hunting party. I think, but am not entirely certain, that helping to butcher animals killed by another man dampens the inherent assertion of superiority of *inkoze* in dealing with someone who has killed when you have not killed. In any case, men are less reluctant to take meat if they have butchered it and men are not reluctant to offer meat to men who help. These meat exchanges are devoid of the dramatic shaming aspect of having to ask for meat and being given the entire kill.

Butchering, an act of labor, is a transformation process mediating between killing and cooking. Women's processing of raw meat into food can be seen as an equivalent and complementary conceptual framework to that of hunting and killing. Men both butcher and cook. If they can use both frameworks then it seems women should be able to use both, yet women do not hunt. Either the answer lies in the conceptualization of fishing and taking small game in or near camp as equivalent activities, available to women but infrequently undertaken, or the role of *inkoze* in defining gender is even more complete than I have allowed.

George helped butcher but did not exercise his claim to the kill, taking only a partial hunting sack of the most fragile cuts and organs. Some internal organs and a few other portions of meat must be utilized shortly after the kill for they do not remain useable without freezing, smoking, drying, or some other form of processing. If Wellington was gaining the power to give away game by his precipitous actions, George was answering with his refusal to divide the game his brother killed. Without trying to plumb their internal mental states or motivations, each can be seen as playing a role in their actions that was directed not just to each other. There was someone beyond the dyad, myself, present at the time of the kill and there was the larger context of the people in camp to play to. In the context of the struggle between them, a solution just between them was without meaning. It was the opinion and affiliation of the wider framework of the audience, the immediate social body to whom their actions were recounted, that they were playing to and for.

After butchering and stacking the caribou in the snow, we went north to the esker where we were to put the tents. We climbed the hill from the south face, a steep climb that becomes a nearly sheer wall and was little used. The first order of business was to build a fire and make tea after which we walked the top of the esker to decide where the tents would go. The top front of the esker had a stretch of open ground that was chosen for the tents. There were two large round boulders, about one hundred feet apart, on the easternmost level part of the clearing and they became the axis upon which the tents were placed. Three people and two boulders. As soon as I verbalized the desirability of having a boulder beside a tent, a rapid assertion of self resulted in a brother in the space adjacent to, and on the inside face of, each boulder. Wellington took the lead again. The most desirable boulder was on the side he faced as the three of us stood in line abreast, and he claimed it for himself. George took the other, which faced him from his position at the north end of the line. Sometimes the only advantage of being in the middle is that you end up in the middle. Paul had left the location of his tent up to his sons, a convenient way to give them first choice and take the least desirable for himself. As always, his position was to take least and demand nothing. By giving, he generated a claim to holding all together with him. His tent was placed behind the north–south axis along the boulders, between and slightly to the rear (west) of Wellington and me.

Wellington went down the east side to the lake shore where he had camped before and recovered the old log tent frames used to support his tent. He carried them to the top of the hill and put up his tent. George, meanwhile, went off and cut logs to build a frame for his tent. I had never built one of these things, and after they had put up their own tents they helped me construct and put up mine. After the tents were up, choosing the location for dog beds was the next concern. George put his in a small cluster of saplings right beside the north side of his tent and Wellington placed his dogs down by the lake shore to the east. He had a bitch and with her puppies had something like sixteen dogs with him. Paul placed his dogs in the open to the southwest of his tent.

The location chosen for the tents was an interesting place in its own right, reflecting a multispecies continuity of judgment with the past. The flat space behind our tents showed dozens of circular rings, scars from tipis of past generations. Each was marked by a ringline where the rim had been and a scar where the central fire had burned inside. Paul liked to show me that the old people had respect for the caribou and had burned their bones. He would take an ax and dig in the sparse dry grass growing where the fire had been and pull out fragments of bone that had been thrown into the fire. He would try to identify the animal the old ones had been eating. The rocks people had carried out to weight down the edges of their tipis were abandoned when they moved. Paul would search in a circular pattern around the ringline for them and pull them up from under the surface growth of moss and lichen. A good place from which to see caribou or other creatures approaching is a good place for any species with that interest. The front slope close by George's tent had been so frequently used by wolves that their old den area, collapsed and filled solid, left an area of habitation remains more visible than the human ones.

After setting the tents we started back toward the cabins and saw two more caribou. They were far away on the ice and wary. We stopped and both Wellington and George shot at them. Having yielded the first kill to his brother, George followed the convention that held the next kill made by the same group to be his no matter who shot it. It was now by matter of right that he shot. Neither of the caribou was killed or knocked down, although there was some discussion as to whether one had been hit.

The arrival of caribou brought hunting to a peak. Everyone was concerned about killing enough to make dry meat for the summer. I spent my time out with Paul who had need of help and another rifle. Wellington and George hunted separately and went farther from camp than their father. He did most of his hunting on the lake ice between the summer and winter camps. Some form of daily hunt or excursion had been the routine for some time. George and Wellington usually tried to get out on the ice just after dawn and, if they found no caribou or sign of caribou, they would take part in excursions like the trip to the river. Now that the hunting had become more serious the daily excursions were forgotten. Paul's demands and needs were less than those of his sons and his experience, greater. His hunts started later and were shorter but timed in such a way that he saw more game than they did.

On May 2, Wellington went off to recover the meat killed the previous day. He let Albert and Mickey follow him on a toy toboggan. They returned to camp shortly, bringing word that Wellington had lost his dogs. He walked into camp, embarrassed at the attention he received and borrowed my snowmobile to go after the dogs. The Chipewyan carry a strong rope on the back of the toboggan that drags behind as they are moving. This is used to tie the dogs when the musher has to leave the team unattended. Wellington had left his dogs for a few moments to go into the bush and had not bothered to tie them. Sure enough, the dogs had seen caribou and had launched themselves in pursuit. He found them on the other side of the lake, a tangled mass of brush, harness, and dog. Paul and I were out hunting and George was off by himself. We had seen Wellington walk over the ice and then go back out, and Paul had figured out what had happened. Wellington was at least spared the embarrassment of our being in camp for his return.

Paul and George were missing the majority of the caribou they fired at on the ice. George was down to his last 50 shells (two- and-a-half boxes). There had been so few caribou moving up the lake, we knew we were catching only an edge of the migration. We later learned the herd had passed a few miles to the west of us along another lake. His inability to kill the caribou he did see was increasingly bothersome to George. He knew, as we all did, that it is hard to judge range accurately as the greyish animals move over the featureless ice. Glare from the slightest sunshine compounded the problem, but these were not adequate reasons. To kill a caribou requires the consent of the caribou, and they do not give this if something is wrong with the hunter or his equipment. In effect, *inkoze* generates knowledge about the state of the hunter and his relationship with the animals on a mystical level that constitutes a comprehensive but unsystematized and diffuse set of pollution beliefs. George feared something or someone had broken the luck on his rifle, that it had become polluted without his knowing how or why. He had a second rifle, a new .30-.06 he was breaking in but his primary weapon was a .303 Enfield, a British ex-military rifle he had used for years. These weapons, slightly modified for civilian use, were relatively cheap[5] and abundant. They were the second most popular rifle among the Chipewyan after the .30-.30 lever-action Winchester. George's fears were for something he had unknowingly done or that had been done to him, but Paul began to develop a series of ideas that the bad luck was a sign of something wrong among kin back in the village. This was a frequent fear on his part consistent with his own structural and sentimental position as father to these men and the most influential man in camp. Paul was looking beyond the group to the wider kin–family situation, while George was looking inside the camp to his own actions or those of someone he should be able to trust.

George's plight was not eased by the events of the next few days. On May 3, Paul shot eight caribou on the lake near camp. He decided this was enough for the summer's dry meat and ceased hunting seriously. The caribou were taken over the lake and left neatly lined up, covered by their own hides. Pieces of plastic bags were tied in the willows that ringed the lake shore to keep scavengers away from the meat. Paul began to focus on the move to the summer camp so May could begin processing the caribou into dry meat.

As if his father's completion of his hunting was not enough, Wellington put on a minor virtuoso performance the same day. He had left on the day's hunt and was well out on the lake before he discovered he had left behind his extra shells. Most civilian rifles carry four shells in the magazine and can carry one in the chamber. The Chipewyan do not trust safeties and do not travel with a shell in the chamber. Extra shells are kept in leather pouches, just large enough to hold a box of shells, carried over the shoulder by a strap and usually decorated with beadwork, fringes, or embroidery. It was this pouch Wellington had forgotten and decided not to return for. He ran into a small bunch of caribou on the lake and was able to kill four of them with the four shells in the rifle. It takes on average, over a season, three shots for each caribou and, since rifles are used for other reasons, six to ten shells are purchased for every caribou brought down. By the end of the day Wellington had decided to join his father in the move to the summer camp so that the making of dry meat could begin. Between the men there had been twenty-three caribou killed with eight already at the summer camp site.

Hunting can be seen to have certain characteristics that are relevant to the developing situation between George and Wellington. Chipewyan men hunt virtually every moment they are in the bush as an adjunct to whatever activity they are engaged in. Killing large game requires the consent of the animal killed and is an aspect of *inkoze* involving, by definition, a brush with the supernatural. A hunt needs to be differentiated from hunting as a specific episode: a bounded, ego-centered, behavioral entity marked off from other activities with no necessary carryover in personnel, other than ego, from episode to episode.[6] A hunt may or may not involve actual sighting or contact with animals but even if no animals are seen, the deliberateness with which it is conducted places the activity within the field of *inkoze*.

Basil Sansom's (1980:3) concept of a "happening," "stands for the form that people bring to the flow of social action to shape it whenever they either present or represent events. Each happening has a typical, almost a classic form, and action that is worth noting or worth gracing with one's own participation is action that is shaped to accord with sets of culturally provided rules that govern proper performance." This concept reveals a crucial aspect of the Chipewyan hunt. The Chipewyan are a people without written language in their daily lives and they deal with the events of their lives through the use of words — verbal representations of events. These representations are not bound by a rigid pattern of formal recounting and rhetoric, but they are nonetheless subject to conventions of cultural patterning. For the Chipewyan, actions exist not only in the "reality" of a describable natural phenomenon but also in the representations of them made back at the camp among their fellows. The conventional representation aspect is important because it is not something that simply occurs after the fact in the telling but is an active part in the experience of the events by the participant. The opposing form the two men adopt in their actions, Wellington's aggressiveness and George's "playing by the rules," are not projections of personality but perceptual stances taken in light of future verbal representations of the events and the attempt to sway the audience for which they are competing.

The rivalry between George and Wellington was diminishing the feeling of common good in the camp and reducing it to its constituent elements. It does not take great imagination to picture the situation in which George now found himself. He was unable to hit the broad side of a barn, yet his father had killed all the caribou he needed, his brother had just killed four with four shots, and both had announced their intention to move to the tents to start the making of dry meat. George's struggle for autonomy was with his brother rather than with his father, so Wellington's actions added more to his anxiety than did Paul's.

## Wellington

Wellington is a large man, five feet eleven inches and of powerful build. He is assertive within a Chipewyan context and an ambitious man, but his ambitions are for economics and independence rather than politics and power. He is almost in microcosm a model of the effects upon the individual of the forces acting within and on his culture. He was in his early thirties in 1975, in many ways the best time of life for expressing the more demanding values of maleness. Intelligent, but always given more to action than thought, he was threading his way through changing times, seeking to use new ways to secure a firm position envisioned largely in terms of old values. To Western eyes the Chipewyan are not an expressive people when it comes to showing emotion, sensitivity, politeness, or concern for others. It is not a question of stoicism but of different values and different ways of expressing them. Beneath these expressions of fortitude and strength is the Chipewyan practice of protecting the self by hiding hurt and desire, but no person can develop an immunity to the frustration and pain of social life. In Wellington they break through in violent outbursts sometimes hidden behind consumption of alcohol.

Some people seem to have a single personality that dominates each role they play or whatever situation they are in, but Wellington has always seemed to me to be many different people. I think him among the most complex of men I have known. Even after I had known him a decade, I never quite felt I could predict his actions. The same man whose passion and temper could break through to harm one child, and endure the stigma for so doing, could spend hours of discomfort trying to catch a baby duck to please yet another one. There is about him a hardness that comes from self-reliance that I am unable to capture. More than any of the others, he is a man trapped in a situation only partly of his own making. The events related here are in large measure the unplanned byproduct of a single gambit of a single spring in the life of this compelling man.

It would be wrong to see him as a man deliberately seeking control over others for I do not believe he ever thought this way. He, like all humans, exists in a social context and the implication and meaning of his actions came not from his intent but from interpretation of his actions by others. He was a strong and purposive man, pursuing his goals in a context where even his simplest and most selfish actions posed a threat to the ability of others to realize their own goals. No human can escape this situation or be judged by the intent of his or her actions. Turning those judgments over to others is among the foremost prices paid for being a social animal.

Wellington's actions after he killed the caribou with four shots only emphasized George's streak of bad luck. When he came back to the camp, Wellington announced what had happened with great delight. He was proud of his accomplishment and told the story several times, on the one hand castigating his stupidity in forgetting his shells while at the same time saying, though not in these words, "look what I did anyway."[7] Genuine appreciation of another person's accomplishment depends at least partly on one's own feelings of confidence, especially if one has to engage in the same activity. George was not particularly confident at that moment, and even though not a word had been said about his own performance, the stellar showing of his brother made him look bad by comparison. He ended the day announcing that he too was finished hunting caribou, saying there was "no point in it."

George's anxiety began to extend into other areas. I can't know when he began to worry about these things but he began to speak to me about them on the previous night. Twice he raised the topic. He spoke about the fish camp and what his brother would do if he got control of it. He feared Wellington was not going to pay him for the guiding work he expected to perform this summer. This was a curious fear, as the fisherman pays the guide separately from any fees paid to the camp. Wellington would not be the person to pay George for guiding even if he did own the camp. What he was worrying about was Wellington's potential abuse of the brother–brother relationship by drawing upon George's more traditional respect for the rules to his own (unfair) advantage. I suggested that Wellington was his brother and would surely pay him for the work. This did not satisfy him. He responded by saying, "Maybe that's why he don't expect me to work for much." It is worth noting that Wellington had a reasonable idea of what was involved in the operation of the fly-in fish camp but had no idea of the advertising, administration, or finances involved. These are hidden parts of the white man's secret knowledge of how things are done. Knowledge of how things are accomplished, in both business and government, is carefully controlled by the northern Canadian white community because this knowledge gives its members their individual positions and power. George had no idea that such things could even exist. To him the outside simply did not exist as other than as names. Even though he had once traveled from Montana to Alaska with me, his experience was not such as to make for a Western understanding of the "outside" a relevant part of his cognitive universe.

George was not without other sources of conflict or at least potential sources of conflict. He was an impulsive person, especially when it came to goods. The previous year he had paid nearly the price of a new snowmobile for a worn-out one. The store was sold out and he did not wish to wait for a new one. It had not lasted the season and now rusted quietly in the village. As soon as he saw the snowmobile I brought into the field, he asked if he could buy it when I left. He was looking for a way to make the money for that purchase. Joan had other plans for the income, real or imagined, of the coming year. She was tired of the small log cabin they used as a home in the village and wanted the money from this year's trapping and wage labor to buy one of the new houses. I certainly thought that a better use of their money, as they were one of the last couples still living in a log cabin. Conflicts over money are not uncommon in marriages and occur most commonly among younger couples. George dealt with some of this frustration by getting Mickey and me to go off goose hunting with him. Whatever the source of his bad luck at caribou hunting, he did not know without experimenting if it carried over to other kinds of game, but he did not take his Enfield.

On May 4 and 5, we started to move to the tents, something that took several days. Each family moved separately, loading their goods onto a dog team, ferrying them past the open water at the neck of the small lake, then over the ice. The ice on South Lake was covered by water in many places and was not safe along the shore or near underwater rock piles. It sometimes seemed like it would have been better to use boats. Not until the evening of the fifth were all the people in the new camp. Paul and May were last to come over. I was more or less attached to them, and we had more to haul than the other families did. The speed of the snowmobile was offset by its greater weight and lesser mobility in the poor conditions. The machine was shared to help each family move. Any major item of equipment should be shared this way.

George broke his run of bad luck on one of these trips. The toboggan attached to the snowmobile has to be steered by someone standing at its back shifting his weight. Even when the toboggan is empty
it should have someone on it. This was one reason George and I had
a slow trip up. Without someone to steer, the toboggan got hung up
too easily and slewed all over the place, even on the lakes. We had
frequently seen caribou moving up the lake in small bands and had
always given chase unsuccessfully. This time we were able to get
close enough for him to kill several. He reacted quickly to his good
fortune, becoming at once more cheerful and throwing himself into
the move with great energy. All concern for what had caused the bad
luck or what might be wrong back at the village seemed to be
forgotten.

Sunday was a good day for George and Paul. I was out helping
them move when we ran into seven caribou. Of the five killed, George
got two. Most of the women and children had been moved and were
busy settling in. Ann, Wellington's wife, had already started to make
dry meat at the old camp, slowing their move to the tents. By now
enough animals had been taken for the people to be more concerned
about converting the raw meat into dry meat than they were about
killing more caribou. A major reason for the move to summer tents
was to get to a place where the ground was clean enough to begin the
butchering and drying. All the men had to build the racks the women
would use to dry the meat and erect the stages to store it.

Wellington had killed more caribou than anyone else but procras-
tinated about bringing it in, losing to wolves not only the four animals on the lake but those killed the day we set the tents. Both George
and Paul ended up with more meat in camp and more converted into
dry meat than did Wellington. Not until they were well into the dry
meat making, did I find out that Ann was very slow at cutting meat
into the thin slabs needed for drying. From what the other women
said, I gathered that Wellington usually was able to kill more than
she could process. If she tried to hurry her efforts, she only ended up
with badly cured meat that soon rotted. Part of Wellington's slowness in bringing in his meat was because he recognized the futility of
the effort. Joan and May were both faster and more skilled than Ann.
The women did not seem to think unkindly of Ann because of her
lack of skill. At least they did not verbally criticize her about it, but

it was not hard to find out that they recognized her deficiency, and there may have been less supportive comments made beyond my hearing.

However artificial the sexual division of labor may be in terms of the actual skills and potential abilities individuals possess, it exerts a real force in social life. Wellington's productivity as a hunter was well known among this group, but the tangible result of his skill was less than that of either his father or brother. His social position was inescapably tied to the skills of his wife. Her slowness seemed to be a product of a genuine lack of skill at a complex and demanding task, but the dependence Wellington had upon her honest exercise of her skills shows how the skill dependence by gender could be manipulated. If Ann had felt hostility or some other emotion she was afraid to show directly, she could have regulated her performance to express it indirectly. Much of Wellington's reputation and social position depended upon her personal behavior. A counter to personal fear is individual action aimed to produce a social consequence. If Ann used such an expression, it would be aimed not at Wellington as a person but at Wellington as a social personality.

The symbolic forms of a culture do not generate uniformity of meaning in individuals but the means by which they can interact without uniformity of meaning at the individual level. The explanations these people offered for the sudden appearance of a waterspout illustrates this and provides a window upon the variations in the way the principal actors saw their world.

Everyone was still settling in when we were disturbed by a strange hissing and gurgling sound. A deep ravine, which began just in front of the northernmost tent (George's), paralleled the axis along which the tents were set, and ended down by the lake on the south side of the point. In a stand of timber at the bottom of this gully there was a small pond still surrounded by snow and covered with ice. The noise came from a column of water about six inches in diameter spurting a foot of so above the ground. This temporary artesian well was very loud and threw the camp into a momentary confusion. As soon as someone was able to locate the source of the noise, there was a general migration down to it.

Wellington decided the waterspout resulted either from a block-
age of the meltwater by the lake ice or from water being forced up
through a connecting passage from South Lake. Saying this, he left,
showing little interest in it. George was inclined to think the water
coming up in the spout might be medicine water and have unusual
properties. He was quite excited by it, staying there until it subsided,
then talking about it all day. He made no attempt to collect any of
the water. Paul would not commit himself, saying it might be medicine water or the result of the ice rising on the main lake.

It was left to May to bring up what we should consider a purely
supernatural explanation. She was the only person in camp to publicly adopt a stance of skepticism toward magical phenomena. It was
not so much that she did not believe in these things as it was that
she could not bring herself to believe that the people she knew, men
her own age or younger, many of whom she had a poor opinion of,
could actually possess this power. Her position was curiously inconsistent. She readily conceded that her dead father had had power,
there were dead senior men she had known who had had great power,
and she even conceded Paul had once had power. In the same breath
she would deny her belief in power and express her fear of it. In the
half-serious, half-joking manner she displayed toward the supernatural, she said maybe it was "a devil coming through." She did not
pursue the subject and no one else picked up on it. As the flow of
water subsided everyone left the area and returned to what they had
been doing. No verbal consensus as to the cause was reached.

The differences between the responses and the explanations did
not come just from each person having a unique personality with
different associations or from each holding a different social position, but from something far more fundamental. These people were
exposed to the same event and did not even recognize it as an event
of the same order of magnitude. Their responses were not one of the
explanation of an event fixed in time and space but of a very different kind, a contexting of the event simultaneously in all three of our
time modes, the past, the present, and the future. They collectively
generated a series of possible explanations that became linked precisely because they were shared and readily available for recall and
comparison with any other event of a similar nature in their experience, be it in their individual pasts and futures or in the verbal and

mythical heritage they share with other Chipewyan. These conflict-ing possible explanations required no resolution because their pub-lic consideration created a unity in which recollection of one aspect reverberated off the total set of explanations that were advanced. Chipewyan explanation is symbolic and serves to build up a series of alternate possibilities that connect aspects of the events into a vari-ety of possible contexts, a widening of possibilities rather than a nar-rowing of them.

A short while after the waterspout subsided and everyone had left, Paul returned to the pond and carefully examined the area. He inspected the orifice from which the spout had come and walked around the entire shore, stopping often to bend down and examine the surface of the ground. Whatever conclusions he drew he kept to himself.

1. The packed snow in the trails freezes readily and it often takes longer for it to melt completely away than it does the surrounding snow. If the snow is melting rapidly, faint traces of the trails are sometimes the last thing to vanish from exposed areas.

2. The dates I give from this point on are correct expressions of time intervals between sets of events but correlation with calendar time is not always as precise. In the bush, calendar time is one of the first things that vanishes from the people's minds and from my notekeeping.

3. Finding yourself crotch deep in wet snow while fending off mosquitoes that seem to be the size of attack helicopters is not only discombobulating but morally offensive.

4. I am reluctant to say "normal" here because what was happening between these two men was perfectly normal. I have been unable to find a better word than "competitive," but must modify the concept so that the striving is recognized without the implication of winning. The adversarial model in our culture is so strong that I know no comfortable way in English to express this striving together against each other.

5. Nothing is ever cheap, except sometimes in quality, in the Hudson's Bay Com-pany store in the village.

6. Woodburn (1982:439) reports what seems to be a similar situation from Africa.

7. The Chuck Yeager phenomenon is not limited to Western man.

# Chapter Five

During the month of May, relations between George and Wellington began to take on the character of an indirect contest. They did not hunt together and rarely took part in joint activities in the bush unless I was along. They became almost openly competitive in little things like making toys or constructing furnishings. The way they went about building floors for their tents later in the month illustrates the tenor of the relations between them. Also during May, wolves became a theme for dealing with the relationships between the men in camp, a motif centered on my own position and interests that did not play itself out until the fall of 1977.

Late in the month of May, my wife had a yen for a wooden floor for our tent. Our youngest daughter was now ten months old, with all the energy and mobility that implies, and was trying to walk. A regular tent floor is made of spruce branches intertwined into a mat and is not very effective at blocking out the chill from the ground, a condition particularly hard on small children. Need does not automatically correlate with skill, and it was beyond mine to make a raised plank floor out of trees using only an ax. Paul needed something to do now that he had finished the dry meat racks and offered to make one for us. Once he began to work on it, Wellington and George, with some persuasion from their wives, decided to make floors for their own tents. They started out to make partial ones for the back part of their tents but soon progressed to full floors. The floors became a topic of conversation among the women, Joan and Ann talking separately to May who became the main conduit between them. There were elements of pride and rivalry in their claims about the floors their husbands were building. In a small camp like this, George and Wellington were acutely aware of what the other was doing. Each heard about the other's floor from his wife and mother, could see how much wood was being brought in, see the pieces being shaped, and see where logs had been cut in the bush.

At the most superficial level the factors that produced this sudden fad were simple and thoroughly harmless. The men were bored and the work kept them busy, the women were given an opportunity for competition through which they could display the solidity of their relationships to their husbands, and most of us stayed a little dryer. There was, however, in this otherwise trivial set of events, an opportunity for George and Wellington to challenge each other, to go head to head in an activity for which they could not be faulted.

Competition between brothers is simply not part of a well-functioning hunting unit. Close kinship should dampen the competition that is built into *inkoze*, and its expression runs counter to both the ideology of the brother–brother relationship and the ideology of shared residence with close kin. However, social cleavage can involve something no more complex than a slight shift from the application of one set of ideas about relationships to that of another equally valid set of ideas about the same relationships. As the month passed, their struggle spread into areas beyond purely male activities and began to draw in more and more people.[1]

The Chipewyan extend the conventions applied to caches and foodstuffs to the property of whites.[2] I have seen Paul allow his family to go hungry rather than take canned goods abandoned at government research sites. George had run out of kerosene for his lamp and wished to get some diesel fuel for it from the fish camp but would not go and take what he needed on his own. Wellington, however, had connections to the camp on several levels: he hoped to gain ownership of it, had worked there for several summers, had the use of a boat and motor from the camp, and had been asked to watch over the camp. George felt this gave his brother the right to take the diesel fuel, and he sought Wellington's permission to take a gallon. On May 6, we made a trip there to get some and Wellington used the occasion to show me around the fish camp.[3] We speculated about the success of his attempt to buy it and the employment opportunities ownership involved.

The following day Paul began to build May's dry meat racks. She was going to dry all her caribou, including pelvic sections, necks, and other bulky parts, and she needed larger and stronger drying racks than the other women. Joan and Ann were already sun-drying their meat. The smoke residue on dry meat upsets some people's stomachs and gives others diarrhea. The use of smoke is a matter of individual taste and negotiation within families. The main reason for smoking the meat while it is drying is to keep flies from laying eggs on it, but with the snow barely gone they were not at the moment much of a problem.

Paul had finished his construction of the first drying and smoking racks and spent the morning hauling meat up from the lake shore. George was also bringing meat up. I was watching the shore and taking pictures, when George saw a caribou trotting by out on the lake. He realized there was a wolf following it. He yelled to Wellington, who came out of his tent with his rifle, while George grabbed his own rifle from his tent. They took the snowmobile and went in pursuit.⁴ The wolf was trailing behind a pregnant cow by some three hundred yards but stopped to eat when he found a gut pile from one of our old kills. The caribou stopped to watch the wolf, turned, then started back toward him before it sensed the snowmobile. The wolf heard the snowmobile (his head was down while he ate and he was facing the other way) and began to run toward an island with brush cover. George and Wellington stopped and shot at him, the wolf turning away from the bullet strikes toward another island. They pursued, finally killing him. He was an immature grey male, most likely one of last year's pups. In the meantime, the caribou had walked back a hundred or so yards toward the snowmobile to see what was going on, and Wellington shot it too.

Killing this wolf created a bit of a situation in the camp. My fondness for the creatures was well known to my companions, but was little reason for them not to pursue an animal with a potentially valuable pelt. The rifle shell tore the young grey badly and its hide had little or no commercial value. The problem was disposing of the hide, the pursuit was automatic. Both of them tried to give it to me but I refused it. I prefer my wolves alive and insisted that since it was killed for its pelt it should not have "died for nothing."⁵ Neither of them really wanted the hide but, after a bit of discussion and jockeying—Wellington killed it, George saw it first, it was my snowmobile—George ended up with the pelt. Later that day we went in pursuit of fourteen caribou we saw on the lake but failed to catch up with them. The final disposition of the wolf's hide was not decided until after this trip as both Wellington and George again tried to get me to take the hide. George finally skinned the wolf and disposed of its remains in the bush where they were not to be found. The hide was drying outside his tent before nightfall.

Pursuit of this wolf was the first time George and Wellington had gone off together in a long time, and it was a special case in that their reaction had to be immediate. Close kinship of this order simply requires that conflict be subordinated in certain situations. That pursuit of a wolf could override their conflict and get them to act together indicates the limited nature of their conflict in the larger scheme of their lives, but their difficulty in deciding what to do with the wolf shows that their conflict was real. They could act and then quibble. One can suppose that if the conflict threatened the existence of the kinship bond itself, they would not be able to act together at all.

The next day was warm and the wind had dropped off. For the first time we could see open water around rocks in the lake and Paul estimated that breakup would occur in three weeks. George and Wellington remained in camp, while Paul went out to pick up some traps from last winter. Joan and Ann separately said they were now going to smoke their meat after it was dry. May had finished cutting a smoke tent for Joan and she was joking about how nice her tent would be. I said, "You should cut a new one for yourself, you always cut them for other people." She laughed and said, "I'm lazy for myself."

Paul took me aside out on the lake ice to tell me (in English) a myth about the caribou and the other animals.

Once Raven captured all the caribou in the world and penned them up behind a fence he had made from their intestinal fat. The caribou couldn't go anywhere. I guess it was six years he kept them in there and all the animals were hungry. The animals all tried to get the caribou out of there, from behind that fence, but Raven had a club. He beat each animal as it tried to break the fence to release the caribou. Wolf, all the small animals tried to make a hole in the fence but Raven beat them all with the club. White fox is fast, the quickest animal. All of the other animals asked him to try and get the caribou out. Finally, he tried it and he was able to make a small hole in the fence. As soon as he did this the caribou were able to get out and run away. Raven flew off, taking their fat with him.[6]

Paul wasn't all that keen on telling myths, so for him to seek me out away from camp to tell me one showed he was concerned with the limits of my understanding in a world where men do kill wolves. I never consciously understood the link between the myth and the point he wished to make about the need to kill, only that it was there. Sometimes, even when facing the strangeness of the other in fieldwork, context and shared experience reveal more than words and logic.

Toy snowmobiles were the rage among the boys. Mike was playing with a new one May had made from an old paper lard box and he had a small paper box he was using as a second snowmobile. Somehow he had found my old hatchet. Fortunately it was very dull and a safer toy than the knife he had had at the cabins. Albert had one too, but it seemed to belong to his younger brother. Mickey was being teased by Paul and May, mostly May, about how bad the insects were going to be in a few weeks. He decided to return to the village at the first opportunity.

May got talking to me about the Eskimo while she cut meat to dry. I mentioned they did not use fire (untrue, but fieldwork sometimes requires certain white lies). She said that she had heard that from Indians in the south and had heard that they made houses from snowbanks and ate their food raw (an insult). She then made a curious connection. She spoke about giving birth in the old days—how Chipewyan women used to have their babies outside on the trail. "They just cut spruce, made a fire, and had the baby. No tent or shelter." She, and the other Chipewyan women, live in a world where Mission teachers' wives can honestly believe (and say) that Indian women feel less pain in childbirth than they do. Chided by Indian women that maybe it's not a question of pain but of greater fear to cry out in a white man's hospital, they are not sure if they should believe such an explanation.

The old practice of having babies on packed snow that May spoke of strikes me as a touch of practical brilliance. The woman delivered from a near upright position so that the force of gravity became an agent helping in the delivery. The snow creates a benign if not sterile environment for the birth and the cold acts directly on the tissues of the woman's body to reduce the chance and severity of hemorrhage.

The camp was in a quiet and reflective mood on the eve of one of the pivotal days in the sequence of events I was following. Thursday, May 8, began in a routine manner. Wellington took his dogs back over to the cabins in the morning to look for something he thought he had left there. The women were busy cutting and hanging dry meat. The children were playing, while the rest of the people were about their various tasks. There was no evidence of caribou passing by, hence the only tasks of any urgency were those of the women.

That afternoon another wolf appeared on the lake, one that probably belonged to the same pack as they grey yearling. Wellington and George took off in pursuit on the snowmobile. I had left the keys in the machine after the confused search for them the last time they needed the snowmobile in a hurry. After a chase of a mile-and-a-half, Wellington shot it. The animal was a large white mature male, which George estimated to be worth nearly $200 at the Hudson's Bay Company store in the village. If he was correct, its estimated value at auction would be close to $400. George had not taken his rifle. The old convention was at work: he had the hide of the first wolf the two of them had killed. Wellington kept the white hide, and this time there was no maneuvering over its disposition. Its remains were also hidden in the bush where they were not to be found.

The day the white wolf was killed Wellington brought up the subject of Joan's earlier appropriation of his supplies and talked about moving from South Lake because of her behavior. He expressed it by saying that he might not stay with his brother because of her actions. Putting it this way indicated that his conflict was with his brother rather than with Joan but that he would express it by placing the responsibility on Joan rather than on his brother. Meanwhile, George was having his own problems. The day before, he had cut his leg with an ax, causing him to walk around stiff-legged. Before this day was over he managed to cut himself again, this time on the thumb. The wound was heavily bandaged and the thumb of his heavy moose-hide glove had been nearly cut off, but the cut healed without incident.

I cannot know how many times his wife's actions had been talked about before today, but George still gave no indication that he knew about either her actions or the talk. Paul and May would not relay stories like this to George, and Wellington or Ann were not about to talk to him about something this sensitive. Joan's actions might not have been entirely unexpected to him, as it is too much to imagine that Joan herself was without dislikes, and her relationship with Wellington was obviously a sore spot. The privacy of the conversations a husband and wife have in their own tent is difficult to get around, but I think it probable that Joan shared her own version of events with her husband and expressed her likes and dislikes to him.

Virtually every act in a Chipewyan life (beyond the solitary excursions of men into the bush) from conception to death, will be witnessed by one or more Chipewyan. The mechanism by which individual actions and behavior are translated into the social fabric is gossip. Gossip is not a brief spotlight that exists for the moment, but is a cumulative residue behind each social personality. Each bit of gossip is eventually pushed from the immediacy of public attention but may resurface intermittently throughout each lifetime and even from beyond the grave.

Gossip plays upon the passiveness of the actor in Chipewyan society (see Introduction) to produce a sense of unease in those individuals subject to its attentions. This unease comes not from the action for which the person is being gossiped about but from the gossip itself. Chipewyan culture does not socialize people to ignore opprobrium. Their sensitivity to being in public view is increased by the teachings of the Roman Catholic Church at Mission. Guilt, sin, and shame are all notions that strike resonant chords in the culture. With responsibility for events placed upon relationships and circumstances external to the actor, gossip usually produces anger and outrage in its subjects. This tends to lead to further actions, with the gossip now held to be the precipitating cause: people begin to do things because of gossip and they cease to do things because of it.

Gossip maintains a moral order, working to keep the values of the community in operation rather than to secure justice for individuals. Moral conduct is thrashed out continuously, with the most recent transgressors serving as negative models. Ideal values tend to be shown, not through the correct conduct of some persons, but through the incorrect conduct all people engage in at one point or another. If the maintenance of the community is achieved at the cost of discomfort, injustice, or even real harm to individual members of the community, that is unfortunate for those persons but essentially irrelevant to the body social.

The gossip system can be manipulated. Unknowing and uncaring, it responds to inventions and falsehoods as readily as to "real" events, such manipulation being a normal part of the system.

Gossip does not provide a trial for the person accused. It does not matter whether the gossip is true or false, just or unjust; its very existence is the sanction. The only victory or justification that can come in a gossip system is the negative one of not being gossiped about, but to escape gossip completely, to be so innocuous as to be above gossip, is to be assigned to a social oblivion akin to death. Even a consensus that a person was justified or falsely accused can only be reached after a humiliating examination of that person's past and present conduct by the community at large. To be accused is to be guilty and punished by the very act of accusation.

Gossip is more than a negative instrument for control and constraint, it is also the instrument by which *inkoze* is established and maintained and by which people rise or fall in esteem within the social system. It is a necessary part of life within this culture and in one sense, gossip is the culture.

Whatever was said about Joan, or whatever she may have told George, the theft of Wellington's goods was one of the few unambiguous forms of retaliation for the resentment she felt that were available to her. Her choice of material objects, something that does not normally excite Chipewyan passions, as a vehicle to get at Wellington was a good one. He was a bit too fond of them for Chipewyan taste. For him to react too strongly over a few foodstuffs could lay him open to allegations of being stingy and greedy himself.

The conflict between the two brothers was submerged in the daily functioning of the camp but there were signs of the trouble. Joan had her new smoke tent in operation and on May 12, it caught fire. The inside of an operating smoke tent is uncomfortable, and Joan had left hers momentarily unattended. The small smoke fire spread from its cleared space to the lichen ground cover and from there to the tent itself. The canvas and the blanket covering the entrance were burned, but most of the meat was saved. When the tent burst into flames most of the adults and all the children rushed over to watch or help. Paul, Wellington, and Ann did not go, and I remained by Paul's tent with them. Wellington cracked jokes as he watched the fire, finally turning back to his own tent with the remark that the meat was "really cooked now."

Earlier that day Paul and I had taken his dog team over to the cabins, the route now impassable to the snowmobile, to get a fish net he wanted his sons to put in the river before the ice became too bad.[7] On the way there he told me he would stay here for the fall and build a new cabin. Statements about "lots of caribou" and "good fish" were followed by his saying that if he trapped right through to Easter he would make "lots of fur." These statements need to be seen as a declaration of position rather than as a serious statement about his intended actions. The argument about trapping until Easter had no reality about it and the characterizations of the fish and caribou were conventional rhetorical expressions of satisfaction with a locale. After nearly sixty years of wresting a living among these very lakes he knew full well that South Lake had become a poor place for caribou and that the lake was one of the worst fish producers around. His statements to me were a counter to Wellington's speculation about leaving because of Joan. Paul was again making an argument for group solidarity and continued co-residence in the face of pressures for separation.[8]

This was the typical pattern of argument and persuasion. Sources of tension and conflict are not faced directly, indeed there is every effort to avoid confrontation. Each person knows that the implication of what is said, if not its exact verbal form, will be conveyed to another person or persons. This mechanism for negotiating decisions keeps all of the adults and older children involved in the decision-making process while avoiding the danger of rupture that can develop from confrontation.

May prepared all of her caribou but cut by cut rather than animal by animal. She had finished preparing the hind legs and tenderloin strips and was now working at deboning the ribs. Her small pet dog had been barking all night, leading her to think the she-wolf that had been mated to the dead white male was close by and searching for him. I said the bitch would have a hard time raising the pups without her mate, but May felt this would be no problem "because wolves always store a lot of meat around the den before the pups are born."

The children had had a terrible day. The Chipewyan do not spank their children very often, preferring threats and stories or failing that, a quick belt.[9] The ritual process of a spanking happened twice today: Mike got one for hitting Albert's little brother with stones and Albert got one for trying to feed my daughter to Wellington's dogs.

Wellington was still taking his dog team out onto the lake ice. Yesterday he stopped out there to untangle one of his dogs, and when he walked forward to the dog he went through the ice. He did not touch bottom, managing to hold on to the ice and pull himself out after being soaked to the waist. This had happened to him before. One spring his loaded toboggan, carrying Ann, Albert, and him, fell completely through the ice. It was only the dogs' fear of being dragged backward into the water that enabled them to pull everyone onto solid ice.

The increasing tension in camp was not something these people would trace to the state of relations between George and Wellington, and there were other things that were more interesting, such as the weather, the lack of caribou, the pending arrival of the insects, immobility and inactivity, than speculating about the state of social relationships. George, Wellington, and I still did things together without my noticing any friction between them, but they were not doing anything together by themselves or with Paul. On a day-to-day basis, the next few weeks in May went reasonably well, the factors affecting our daily life well within the bounds of normality. The lake ice continued to deteriorate and the toboggans were now used with one of the fish camp's aluminum boats slung on top. The boat was an emergency device in case the ice gave way, and it could be untied to use where there was enough open water to make it worthwhile.

In time the water opened along the shore all the way around the lake and we could get around in the boat. By the end of May the dogs were no longer being used, and all travel was on foot or by boat. The caribou had all passed except for a few animals straggling through the bush after the herd. There was talk that some of the bulls might remain in the forest for the summer but we saw no sign of this. The Chipewyan are an active outdoor people and the most basic problem for the men was that they did not really have enough to do to keep

busy. The warming weather and increasing insect population aggra-
vated their situation.

The wolf pack was still in the area and it made the camp restless
the nights of the twelfth and thirteenth. The wolves themselves were
barely noticeable, but the dogs were scared and made a racket all
night. George and Wellington were talking of going out and finding
the den to collect some of the pups. This had an aura of compensat-
ing me for the killing of the two wolves mixed with some talk of
raising the pups as sled dogs. It was not a serious gesture, provoked
more by the inactivity of the breakup season than by anything else.
It soon died out.

There was now a running discussion over whether to stay at South
Lake or move somewhere else. By May 13, people were openly talking of moving north to Foxholm Lake after breakup. Wellington
opposed this strongly,[10] saying he was staying at South Lake no matter what anyone else did. This was a reversal of his speculation the
day of the white wolf kill. Statements like this need to be seen as
honest expressions of the feelings of the moment rather than considered attempts at manipulation. Emotion "confuses" categories, as
Durkheim and Mauss (1963:5, 87) have argued, but emotions, however fleeting, expressed in a situation like this are themselves generated by categorical systems with their own internal logic and are
indirect expressions of power in social relationships.

The women still had a few tasks related to the dry meat but only
May was doing anything major. She had decided to make grease from
the caribou leg bone marrow and, much to their disgust, the children had to be banned from her work area. The chance of them getting burned was too great. Both little Ann and Mickey were in need
of glasses. Mickey was hopelessly nearsighted and had broken his
only pair. About his only other entertainment was to go off with the
.22 to shoot at birds or other convenient targets. Paul and May hated
to deny him the .22, but the ricochets and stray bullets from his poor
target identification were a threat to the entire camp. Eventually he
was given free access to the .22, but the shells were hidden and he
was told they had run out.

While we were out on one of our jaunts, Wellington noticed that
George kept his sugar, tea, and tobacco wrapped in small pouches of
clear plastic. George proudly told him his wife packed his lunch and

wrapped these things in individually prepared measures to protect them. Wellington roared with laughter at this and began to tease him. What George presented as the actions of a good wife, carefully measuring out a day's supply of goods at a time to make them last, was represented by Wellington as the mark of a henpecked husband who let his wife dole out trivial portions. What kind of a man was George that he let his wife control their supplies and parcel them out in insultingly small quantities like he was a child? This was a touchy point. George did not know exactly just what was in his tent. With his wife's reputation for stinginess, the point went heavily to Wellington.

One of the women explained to me how she thought Joan managed to keep the knowledge about their supplies from George. This woman had teased George, saying he could look in Joan's suitcase to see what supplies were in there if he were not afraid of her dirty underwear. She was teasing him about his fastidiousness, but to George the issue was pollution. It seems that Joan did keep certain of their supplies like tea, sugar, and tobacco in a suitcase. She also kept part of her clothing, in particular her underwear, in that suitcase. Women's underpants are exposed to menstrual fluids and are considered polluted by that contact. The pollution is also considered to be contagious. George was unwilling to open any suitcase but his own, for to do so might bring him into contact with a polluted garment and so put him into a state offensive to the game animals he hunted. After his string of bad luck in the spring he was not about to risk any such action. The woman who told me this was impressed by Joan's ingenuity and displayed a condescending humor at George's gullibility. She was totally unaware of his concern for pollution beliefs—a classic example of how gender differences can lead people to interpret the same situation in a compatible manner without realizing that their understanding of the relevant causal mechanisms underlying the situation are different.

By the seventeenth, there were expressions of concern for the remaining family members back at the village and thoughts of the supplies that could be obtained there. There was no possibility of contact with the village now. The remaining ice would not support aircraft on skis, and shattered ice floes prevented float planes from landing. Long distance travel by boat or dog was out of the question, so any movement to the village would have to be on foot. Wellington was curious about the future of the fish camp and everyone accepted that he would have to go there when air travel again became feasible, but someone else would have to go for supplies. The people were negotiating who else should go back to the village. Everyone was ready for a break and wanted to go, but the cost was prohibitive.

Paul had even gone so far as to say that he might go on to Foxholm Lake in June and leave Wellington and George at South Lake to work at the fish camp. He seemed to think their families would go with him and his sons could come up after the guiding season. He did not seem to realize that both Wellington and George felt he was only marginally capable of being left alone in the bush for very long. If he went to Foxholm Lake, one or the other of them would have to go with him. George's preference for places happened to coincide more closely with his father's than did Wellington's, and he was more sensitive and more inclined to accommodate his father.

On one of our earlier trips, using dogs to pull a boat on top of a toboggan, we had gone down to the river at the south end of the lake. We wanted to see if the water was open and if there was any game to be found. We spent some time shooting at a loon and saw grizzly bear tracks. On the way back Wellington let loose one of his dogs because it would not pull in harness. On the night of the nineteenth, the same dog "was drooling, not eating, biting at trees, stumbling, growling, showing extreme fear mixed with aggression" (fieldnotes). Wellington noticed it while he was feeding the dogs and called to me as I passed by on my way to get water. He was concerned but convinced the animal could not escape from its chain. We decided to leave it overnight and, with heavy persuasion from me, shoot it in the morning if it was still sick. I was afraid it might have rabies or distemper, which could spread to the other dogs.

Dogs play a special role in Canadian Northern Athapaskan cosmology, and there is a historical–mythical dimension to the relationship between people and dogs, as belief in a dog origin was widespread. Dogs serve in not so subtle ways as indicators of a man's social position and relationship to other people. Savishinsky's (1975) work, among the distant but related Hare Indians, shows that a man's treatment of his dogs reveals a great deal about his self-image. The Mission Chipewyan use dogs as symbols in a series of metaphors about gender and relations between humans, and this usage reflects *inkoze*. There is a special relationship between a man and the women attached to him, particularly his wife, that is reflected by and causally linked to his dogs and the way he treats them. Most Chipewyan do not like to shoot dogs, so I reluctantly offered to shoot Wellington's dog for him the following morning, as its condition had deteriorated. It was in character that Wellington refused my offer and shot the animal himself. I soaked the remains in diesel fuel and burned them along with the area surrounding the dog's bed. The burning had to be repeated to sanitize the remains, but the illness did not spread to the other animals.

The symbolic load carried by dogs was such that this incident added to the camp's anxiety level. Fortunately it had not been one of George's or Paul's dogs. Their interpretation of an event like this would have added even more to the camp's concern than did Wellington's matter-of-fact approach. As with the dead fox in April, the killing of the dog was not so much a cause of anxiety in itself but rather something picked up on because of the other worries in the camp.

The days between May 20 and May 27 were quiet. The mosquitoes were out in full force and any trip into the bush had to take account of these beasties. They were quite effective in curtailing activity. It was especially hard for the women to get away from the tents, as they had to deal not only with the insects but with the children who were extremely hard pressed by the bugs. There was enough open water for the men to get around in the boat and we were able to entertain ourselves by going fishing. The fish have a voracious appetite in the long spring days and warmer weather. Female jackfish (northern pike) come up into very shallow water near beds of reeds and can often be seen, as their fins and part of their backs stick out of the water. The choice locations are taken by fish in the thirty to thirty-five pound range. The people say wolves and other animals sometimes hunt them from the shore this time of year.

The women had finished the dry meat and had a lot of free time for other activities. The first berry picking of the year was just underway. They would arrange for one of the men to go along with them after muskeg berries. Before they ripen, these berries are firm and tart, but after ripening they become soft and tasteless. Joan was being excluded from their activities by the other women, so George took

her out to help her pick berries. This was a double statement upon
the state of social relations in the camp. Whichever man took the
other women out would wander off to do something else or pick berries for himself without contributing to the pots the women filled
for use back at the tents.[11]

The shortage of supplies was making itself felt, with tobacco the
most missed item. The Chipewyan are well used to doing without
the small material luxuries that make life more pleasant but their
absence is aggravating. Everyone had publicly said they were out of
tobacco. Paul and May said it because they actually were out of
tobacco, but every one else meant that they were low on fresh cigarette tobacco. The local supply had already been recycled, the floor-
boards in the cabins raised to gather cigarette butts thrown in past
seasons onto the floor to fall beneath to the sand and burn themselves out. The tobacco from these was mixed with fresh tobacco to
produce a strong and pungent rolling tobacco. There was talk of trying the old tobacco substitutes, but no one really wanted to smoke
willow bark or any of the other plants that were used to stretch
tobacco. At one point May experimented with a concoction of fried
snuff and muskeg berry leaves but no one had the nerve to smoke it.

The tobacco shortage became another arena of competition
between George and Wellington. Wellington had a supply of the less
expensive pipe tobacco that had been purchased for an occasion like
this. There were rumors of a private stash for himself and Ann based
on stories of them sitting inside their tent smoking. It was a little
less clear what George's "out of tobacco" meant. The going interpretation was that Joan had locked it in her suitcase and he didn't know
how much there was. People thought that she told him how much
they had but that she lied. When he got some to give to his parents,
Wellington followed the gift with a larger one of his own.

To hide the possession of something like tobacco is possible but
to hide its consumption is impossible. The children run freely among
the dwellings with an almost total disregard of the current state of
the relations between the adults. They carry word of who is, and
who is not, consuming what throughout camp. In the case of tobacco
there were marginal people like little Ann who smoked but were not
regarded as adults. She had no means to purchase a supply adequate
for the months of isolation. No one would give her tobacco of her

own and only sometimes would the women let her have a cigarette. She was forced to pick up whatever butts she could find and to steal tobacco whenever opportunity presented itself. She had the most acute sense of any one in camp of who did and did not consume tobacco, just how much they consumed, and when they did it. The upshot of all this information passing among the people about the supply of this item was to place George in a position where he began to look a little ridiculous. He seemed not to know that his brother was matching and surpassing his own gifts of tobacco to their parents. There was no reason for him not to know save his own social ineptness or to hide a lack of control over his own tobacco supplies. His brother's simple gifts weakened George's social position by spotlighting the poor opinion of his wife that was held by the other women and older children. The conflict was generated by the clash between kinship ideology and the ideology of egalitarianism intersecting the position the two men occupied in their respective life cycles, but now that the caribou hunting was finished, Joan's status had become the focal point for the definition of George's position.

## Joan

Joan is a tall angular woman in her mid-twenties who is extremely shy around strangers. Curious and given to thoughts of adventurous fantasy, she is not a particularly intelligent woman. She has little inclination, or ability, to read social situations and act in such a way as to minimize her discomfort. She often played into the hands of others by doing things that increased her own isolation and discomfort. Not until 1983 was she relaxed enough in my presence to freely engage in conversation. Even more than Ann, I must judge her from her actions and what was said about her.

Youngest in a family that had had more than its share of male deaths, she was a favored child. As is often the case in systems with even the strongest conceptual distinctions between male and female, the behavior of real individuals reflects many factors other than categorical relationships. Joan was able to engage in many activities normally the province of males and was, in the archaic term of our culture, a perfectly normal tomboy.

Joan's father and Paul were such close friends that they invented fictive kin ties in lieu of real ones. She grew up having frequent contact with Paul's family and children. As George established himself as an eligible bachelor, Joan's father approached Paul with the suggestion that a marriage be arranged between Joan and George. In time Paul agreed and a match was arranged. With the characteristic affinal kinship terminology applied after this marriage, Paul and Joan's father were suddenly *seri* (same generation, same gender, related by marriage); no longer fictive kin but related by one of the closest of all Chipewyan relationships.

Paul's acceptance of the proposal for his son's hand met no opposition from May. Everyone, Joan, Paul, May, Fred, Joan's parents and siblings, initially approved the match—everyone but George. His opposition to it then brought him support from his siblings but to no avail. He married Joan out of respect for his parents but living with her was something else. He refused to do so for months. By the time this issue was resolved, there was such a backlog of bad memories, hurt, rumor, and conflict between the two of them that it was difficult for them to develop a solid relationship. By 1975, after the birth of their second child, their relationship had evolved into a stable arrangement. George had developed a great affection for his wife as well as the healthy dose of respect due her strong personality. His willingness to break from his brother and risk a break with his parents must be seen in some measure as reflecting his respect and affection for his wife. I do not know what Joan's feelings for her husband were at this time, save that they were still tinged by past hurt, but her actions were those of a willing but strong-willed wife.

Joan's position in the camp was not comfortable and her transition from highly-esteemed daughter to marginal, almost outcast, wife cannot have been an easy one. All the women but May were hostile toward her and this was expressed in gossip and exclusion from their activities. Her social contact was limited largely to Paul, May, George, and the children of the camp. Joan could turn only to Paul and May for sympathy and support outside her conjugal family. They had arranged the marriage that brought her to live among them and did not like the disapproval their children expressed, but they were not able to do much to make Joan's life more comfortable. They were caught between their own children and not so blinded by their fussing as to miss Joan's real faults.

On May 28, Wellington began to tell several brilliantly constructed stories, which amounted to an attack on George at his weakest point: his wife and her sexuality. Little Ann was included in a peripheral incident, otherwise they involved only Wellington and Joan. Little Ann's accounts were so garbled and inconsistent that I do not know if she in fact saw what she was supposed to have seen or if she was merely saying what she thought she was supposed to say. It would add substance to the tales if they happened to be true, but their form and telling is the issue, not their veracity.

The first story was supposed to have happened while George was out in the bush on May 28. Wellington was on the way down the hill to feed his dogs. To get to them he followed the path north past the other tents then east down a steep slope to the lake shore. This was the easiest route to the lake and was used by the entire camp. Joan looked out of her tent and saw Wellington coming, whereupon she popped back inside and grabbed a container of waste water. By the time she had done this Wellington had passed her tent. Joan ran down the hill in front of him and threw the water on the ground. She then asked where he was going. Upon being told he was going to feed his dogs, she walked back up the hill, laughing loudly all the way to her tent.

The second story was told on May 29 about an incident that was supposed to have happened earlier in the day. Wellington was again on his way down to feed his dogs when Joan saw him from her tent. Before he passed, she came outside and went into a small depression a few yards northeast. No one had bothered to build outhouses at the tent camp, and certain areas quickly became known as places to relieve yourself.[12] The depression Joan entered had no sheltering vegetation, its privacy came only from its being below eye-level from the camp. Just before Wellington passed in front of her tent, Joan dropped her pants, squatted, and urinated where he could not help but see her.

Stories take time to spread even in a small camp, and Wellington had to tell them several times. He developed in their telling a very effective device to deal with Joan's squatting, a plaintive, "Why she wanna do that in front of me?" He used an English phrase, "I didn't say nothing," which is a rhetorical device for asserting that actions in the face of provocation have been highly correct. He liked these stories so much that he added a third, previously unmentioned, one. That story referred to an earlier time during which Joan had urinated as Wellington and little Ann returned from looking for the tracks of a bogeyman little Ann said she had seen waving to her from the lake shore.

The stories were properly scandalous and their connotations were unquestionably sexual. Joan was accused of breaking a series of conventions of modesty in an overt and forceful way. The Chipewyan are not verbally reticent about human sexuality but are ambivalent about individual sexuality. They are most emphatically disconcerted by female sexuality at the symbolic level. In the third story the sighting of a bogeyman added to the sexual tone, as bogeymen are most frequently seen by girls and unmarried women at times when the socialization of their sexuality and gender roles are most liminal and negotiable. To make things worse, or perhaps more accurately, to recognize Wellington's skill in manipulating a verbal form, siblings-in-law are in a category such that sexual relations between them should be regarded as incestuous. They are also the category of nonblood kin with whom the physical opportunity to engage in clandestine sexual alliances is greatest.

Gossip of Joan's somewhat checkered sexual history between the time of her marriage and George's assumption of co-residency gave an inherent plausibility to the stories. By assuming the position of the innocent but moral man, striking at the ambiguous and dangerous sexuality of an affinal woman, Wellington delivered a telling blow. In that a conventional response to an allegation of sexual misconduct on the part of one's spouse is conflict, often leading to a physical fight, Joan herself now had reason to keep the stories from George even if they were pure fabrications.

The stories spread among the adults and older children, and I am sure Joan knew of them. I have no indication they ever reached George. The subtlety of the attack on George played on the ribald in the Chipewyan sense of humor and allowed Paul and May to enjoy them without having to become angry. It was hard for them not to be amused at the stories, yet they would have reacted quickly to a direct attack on George. They would have invoked the weight of their parental legitimacy and authority to preserve the group structure and restrain the conflict rather than become involved in a judgment upon the specifics of the dispute. With the raising of the spectre of the legitimacy of his wife's sexuality, George's position deteriorated to the point that I do not see how any effective counter was possible.

He remained popular, personally more popular than Wellington, but he was reduced to near-impotence in the debate over his wife's actions and character.

The weather was typical of a mild subarctic spring at the end of May. The twenty-third was the fourth warm day of bright sunshine. Forest fire season had already begun and in the clear air we could see smudges of smoke looming over the horizon from the fires to the south. An attempt was made to determine where the fires were and how severe they might be. On May 24 and 25, I took advantage of the six inches of fresh snow to haul in a few weeks' wood supply with the snowmobile. Subsistence activity was down to some desultory fishing and duck hunting, and everyone moped about the lack of tobacco and tea and hoped a plane would come soon. The lake ice had broken into sections, so we could take the boat out, floating it between the floes then pulling it up onto the larger sections and sliding it over them. Tricky business that: the boat will slide over ice that a person will fall right through. Paul resurrected his idea of making a forty mile trip to one of his old cabins where there were "seven cans" of cigarette butts left from several years ago. Nobody took him too seriously. Even in his prime he would have been hard put to survive such a trip by himself in conditions like these.

Anticipation of an airplane arriving mounted steadily and as ice-free water came nearer, so did the tourist fishing season. George's ambivalence about staying was again obvious. He talked about going to Foxholm Lake at breakup even while he worried about how much Wellington would pay him for working at the fish camp. Staying at South Lake was tied to Wellington's social position, that much had been accomplished in the last few months, while George's autonomy was associated with his leaving. Paul had decided that he and May had to return to the village to get supplies and check on the rest of the family. This would, coincidentally, give him a temporary respite from the stress of the camp and postpone a decision about moving to Foxholm Lake. The decision he and I made about our location for the fall camps would be critical to George's immediate hope of autonomy. The lack of purpose and sense of waiting continued until June 5, 1975, when an airplane finally arrived.

The aircraft was a harbinger of change, but little of its news was good. The plane had some tobacco on board that had been sent up to us, so that issue was resolved, but the aircraft was not for us. It was from the main tourist lodge and carried word there were to be only a few days work for George and Wellington, preparing the camp for the two-week occupancy of the one couple that was coming up to fish. Wellington would have a further two weeks of work guiding but there would be no guiding for George. The fish camp was to remain in the hands of its present owners. Wellington's application for a loan had either been denied or it had not been adequately followed up. In effect, Wellington had been euchred into coming to watch over the camp at his own expense.

The loss of Wellington's bid to control the fish camp was a deadly blow to his chances of constructing a hunting unit around himself that included his father and his brother. This was the point when his bid for influence collapsed, although it did not seem that way at the time. In the traditional system of the Chipewyan, leaders were able to attract adherents because they were men who so understood the bush they were able to make skilled decisions about locations that led them to food (D. M. Smith 1982). As their skill was displayed over time, less skilled judges of the environment—I am not considering the social environment—followed their lead. That is precisely what Wellington was doing with the fish camp: it was a resource, but his judgment about it had been incorrect. He could stay, he could get what he wanted here, but the others could not and they would not stay with him.

1. The process of change in these people's relationships soon came to be caught within larger social changes in their world as economic and social pressures from the outside forced the conjugal family to assume a role more like the ideological norm in the rest of Canada.

2. In 1911, the famous naturalist Ernest Thompson Seton said in *The Arctic Prairies*, (1981:147) "These Chipewyans are dirty, shiftless, improvident, and absolutely honest." The tone and tenor of his view are not dissimilar to those the Chipewyan confront in much of white Canada today. The Chipewyan do sometimes get dirty, so Seton was one for four.

3. The fish camp itself was a simple entity consisting of, "two plywood tent frame buildings, (one sleeping six people, three bunks, one eating). Crude plywood–spruce tables, school chairs and logs (seats), two boats, one at (Wellington's), one motor, two in town. Total value $3,500 max. in (Parklund), here $9,000" (fieldnotes, names changed).

4. They asked permission from my wife because I had not left the keys in the machine as was my custom and it took her a few moments to find them.

5. Refusing a gift is breaking the one universal bit of advice given all anthropologists during their graduate education. Time and familiarity allow the bending of rules. These people knew I had a thing about wolves and interpreted it in their own way, generally accepting it as a normal part of my behavior. As I had to adjust to them, so they had to adjust to me. It is never a one way process.

6. Paul's English is limited and heavily influenced by Chipewyan stylistic and grammatical conventions. I have put his version into a form more familiar to the general reader.

7. They didn't. He wanted them to put his net in the water far beyond the distance he could travel to check it himself. The net and its potential fish yield were irrelevant; their cooperation in a task for the common good was what was important. The fish were to be used as dog food, so again a canid metaphor — feeding dogs — was being used to make a statement — cooperation and sharing food — about human social relations.

8. The cost of purchasing and transporting sufficient supplies for a stay of this length was well beyond Paul's (or my) financial means. Even if he had been able to arrange the financing, May would never have agreed to miss the Christmas season when all of her children and their families would be in the village.

9. Chipewyan women sometimes settle disputes with their small children by engaging in a "fight" rather than spank them. This sounds horrendous to a Western reader until one realizes that the process of losing a fight to a larger and more powerful adult leaves the child with the dignity of having been treated as an equal in a contest and the honor of actively protesting the adult's actions. Because of the size disparity the fight is quick and controlled with less damage delivered to the child than there is in a Western spanking.

10. His overall position was entirely consistent. From the beginning he made it clear that, while he preferred us to be with him, he was going to South Lake and we could go where we chose to go.

11. That men do not pick berries for common consumption is not a rule but a generalization formed from repeated observations over the years.

12. One of the ambiguities of camp life among a people very sensitive to nakedness (Beidelman 1961, 1968, 1971; Fortune 1932, 1936) is making sure the area of bush used as a toilet is not occupied when you go to use it. The people in each tent used the closest secluded place; George, to the north of his tent; Wellington, in the woods toward the small pond and the woods to the south of his tent; Paul and I on the other side of the same woods along the top of the high bank to the south shore. When the mosquitoes and black flies are in full force, speed of elimination is of the essence. Outbreaks of diarrhea during insect season can produce strange conventions of privacy.

# Chapter Six

Wellington and George have received the lion's share of attention here, but that should not be taken to mean that they or their actions dominated the life of this camp. To analyze a situation or a whole society as a function of a singular aspect of that whole is a powerful analytical method, particularly if it is an underlying aspect (Huber 1980:45), but these people were going about the business of living their lives in a perfectly ordinary manner, the conflict between George and Wellington generally far from their minds. I have tried to indicate this and provide a glimpse of what normal life was like. From this point onward the cast of characters will become more varied as people begin to move around. Concomitantly, the analysis will shift increasingly to the actions of specific individuals, but this increasing specificity should not be taken to indicate a change in the nature of daily life. Eventually this camp will split and the narrative will beome less linear in its structure.

The arrival of the aircraft on June 5, 1975, set off a flurry of activity. After the pilot gave George and Wellington the list of things to be done at the fish camp he flew up to our place and landed. As Paul and May made ready to board the aircraft it became apparent there was going to be a space problem. Their dependent children had to go out with them. George and Joan's infant son had become ill and needed medical attention so he had to go too. Mickey was so anxious to leave that he was standing by the plane, packed, not speaking to anyone. I suggested he wait until the next plane came on Saturday at which point he scrambled onto the float, went down it to the door and then went inside. To the amusement of everyone, he refused to budge. I couldn't resist asking May, so Mickey could hear, why he had to go now. She responded saying, "I don't know." I then asked why she didn't tell him to come out of the plane. She looked at him, shook her head, and said, "I can't get him out of there." By asserting his will in a crucial situation Mickey had already well relearned a major feature of his culture. His determination generated a bemused but approving laughter from the adults standing outside the plane, and they made room around him for those going south.

In the course of the aircraft's coming and going we received word that the Old Black Woman had died. She had had a number of friends among us and we were saddened by the news of her death. She had been unable to keep down any food, weakened, and died. The people accepted her own explanation of her pending death and attributed it to starvation. News of her death prompted George to tell me about noises he had heard coming from inside her cabin which he had shown me on Missionary Lake. He had stopped to spend a few nights at his father-in-law's cabin in the otherwise deserted settlement when he heard something moving about in her cabin. His investigaton revealed nothing that could have made the noises. He returned to his cabin only to hear the noises once more. He again looked in her cabin but could not find anything. Knowing it could not be mice or squirrels, he did not return the next times he heard the noises. When he heard of her death he realized that the noises had been made by an aspect of her spirit making a last visit to places she had loved dearly but would not see again "in this world." His failure to understand what the noises had been distressed him and he said that he would never again fail to recognize this situation.

June 6 and 7 were spent preparing the fish camp. We did not have the tools to make the repairs it needed, so it had to settle for some touch-up painting and a good cleaning. The dock was falling apart, but the camp's management would pay Wellington only half a day's wages to repair it. To have put it into a safe condition would have taken Wellington and George several days. After an hour or so of work, Wellington managed to make it look repaired. Right now he felt about as much obligation to the owners of the camp as they had shown to him. He explained cheerfully that he was not doing what they had said he should do and was not taking as long as they had said he should take to do it. After the final day's work, George came to my tent to grouse about Wellington, saying he was stingy and often

cheated him. George was still thinking about moving to Foxholm
Lake and knew that if he stayed here he faced a period of idleness
when the tourists came.

After the chores were finished at the fish camp on June 7, the rest
of the day was spent waiting for the fishermen to arrive. Their plane
came over South Lake in the evening, and the three of us got the boat
and went down to meet them. We were expecting the plane, and the
dogs heard it before it was in sight, so we had time to get down there
before the pilot could circle around and land. We stood on the shore
and watched the plane idle into the beach ignoring the dock
Wellington had repaired. The first person out of the aircraft was
Corky. He stepped onto the float and then hopped to shore while
engaging us in animated conversation. His wife emerged onto the
float and watched a bit before asking him to help her get to shore.

Corky was in his midthirties, a dishwater blond of average height
and build. His wife was tall, blond, attractive, about thirty, and a bit
unsure of herself. Even before she had had a chance to speak, Corky
had told us her name, that she was his second wife, and that she had
borne him a son the year before. He was obviously proud of her, but
spoke about her in a way that reminded me of the way he spoke of
his Panthera automobile or his hunting trophies. She, whether she
liked it or not, was on display. Her request for Corky's assistance in
getting off the float was denied with his assurances that she could do
it herself. After a few moments, when it became clear that he was
not going to help her, she jumped only to fall on her backside at the
waterline.

Both of them were nervous about their adventure. A week deep in
the wilderness, far removed from the amenities of civilization, is a
thing many people dream of but few are ready for or able to face if
the opportunity ever arises. They proved to be engaging people, both
well-behaved and decent, who got along well under what could have
been intimidating circumstances.

Corky was a self-made millionaire who had earned his wealth
before he reached thirty. He had founded and franchised a chain of
insect extermination businesses in the eastern Midwest. He was very
much the high-powered achiever and was paying the price for it.
Wracked by tension, he took heavy doses of pain relievers and
antiinflammatory drugs to counteract the effects of stress upon his

back. Even here, on a rare vacation, he was daily immobilized by back spasms. Somehow, after making his fortune, he had found time to go back to night school at the University of Cincinnati and complete his B.A. During his education he had acquired an interest in Atlantis, Mu, and other comparable ideas. One of the these ideas was the Bigfoot or Sasquatch.[1]

Corky and Wellington knew each other from the previous summer's fishing and had established a genuine and lasting relationship involving mutual affection and respect as well as economic exchanges. Corky had tipped him well and given a substantial bonus in the form of fishing gear. Chipewyan guides value highly any gifts from their tourist. For many of these men, guiding is an expression of their personality and competence. Giving gifts is a one-way process however, from client to guide. This relationship was unlike any other I have ever seen between fisherman and guide. Wellington had frequently talked about Corky in the spring and was later to involve him in activities that transcended both norms and legality. Wellington gave Corky the white wolf hide. The gifts Corky gave Wellington were genuine but trivial compared with his resources; Wellington's gift of a wolf hide worth $200 or more was equally genuine but not trivial.[2]

Corky and his wife seemed relieved by my presence, taking it as reassurance that contact with the outside world was possible. We had a high-frequency radio in our camp, but no one had the heart to tell them that it had never worked. After Wellington made arrangements to pick them up for the next day's fishing, he armed them with a rifle as we were leaving. They were worried about bear, and hearing of our discovery of grizzly tracks in the spring didn't make them feel any better. The topography of the area was such that any large animal swimming that part of the lake would cross the island and pass by their tent. The rifle could be heard from our camp in all but the worst weather and was intended as a signaling device rather than as a means of protection.[3]

Early each morning Wellington would go down to their camp and take them fishing. Late each evening he would take them back there and return to our camp. There is useable daylight until nearly 11:00 P.M. in early June, and dawn comes only a few hours later. A day's fishing generally exceeded twelve hours except when it rained. Corky was a talkative man and while they fished he got to telling stories.

Many of the stories had to do with various beasts and beasties to be found in the wilderness and one of the beasties was the Bigfoot.

Wellington would return home full of the events of each day's fishing and tell the stories he had heard. He first told them to Ann, but his own and other people's children overheard them. This was a selection process at work. Wellington picked out the incidents and stories that most struck him and later responded to his audience's requests for details. Any incident or story that struck someone's fancy was retold to other people by the listener. With each telling the narrator was free to take the story further and further from what Wellington himself had said.

The Bigfoot was by far the most popular of the stories. After his return, Paul would quickly make the translation of Bigfoot into Chipewyan: *bekaycho, be* (third person singular, no gender distinction); *kay* (foot); *cho* (large). Both the English and the Chipewyan words were used even by small children. These stories bounced around the camp, mostly from child to child. The children would go to the adults seeking clarification of details or verification of the authenticity of versions or parts of versions. They talked about Bigfoot among themselves and were little constrained by what Wellington had originally heard from Corky.

One independent source of verification for these stories came from my eldest daughter and was carried back to the adults. She was just four at the time and like most of her generation, a child of television. In the early 1970s a car dealership in Vancouver, owned by a man named Basil Plimley, advertised heavily on television. Many of its commercials were produced by local agencies and centered on the person of the owner. One advertisement which she had seen many times before our trip north, had Mr. Plimley standing on a road she knew that led into a local ski area in Mt. Seymour Park. A short distance from Mr. Plimley sat the particular model car he was trying to sell. As he began to speak of the virtues of that particular model, left so carelessly unattended, the camera shifted up the mountain behind him. He, but not his voice, vanished as a prototypical Vancouver snowbunny was pursued down the ski slope by a large and clumsy monster with huge feet, long white hair, and an odd face. The woman reached the car, climbed in, and escaped by driving out of the picture. The pursuing monster stepped on a toboggan and slid out of the picture. At the end of the sequence, Mr. Plimley, the car, and the woman were back on screen, followed by the demise of the monster, at which point the action part of the commercial ended.

When the other children began to speak of the Bigfoot, my daughter responded that of course it was real because she had seen it on television. Her statements went to her playmates and from them to their parents. That she saw Bigfoot on television had no particular authority among these people. I think all the adults had seen television by 1975, but none of them had had much exposure to it or thought of it as anything other than a desirable novelty. What did matter was that her statements confirmed Bigfoot's existence, to the extent a four year old's statements are taken seriously, and provided another occasion for the stories to be retold vertically through the generations.

A single exposure to virtually anything new can be shrugged off, but things that are real tend not to come in a single exposure. There is an incremental increase in exposure as separate aspects of the new reality are discerned and discussed. This was one conspicuous feature of the introduction of Bigfoot, the steady accumulation of incidents and events that added new dimensions, each of which created a new occasion to talk about *bekaycho* and to retell the stories.

Wellington always presented Corky's stories as Corky's stories rather than ones that Wellington himself vouched for. He did know bogeyman stories, could tell them, and would explain them to me if I asked about them. When asked if bogeymen were real, he would either take the traditional male position, saying, "I never seen one" or laugh and say that of course they were real. Either choice could be made, especially when other men were standing around in the village and could all grin at each other.

I was not entirely sure how to react to the stories of Bigfoot. After a certain amount of experience it is possible to recognize a forming situation that is worth investigation, but I promptly fell under the old illusion of thinking that I had to minimize my own influence to make the situation more natural. I adopted the stance I had heard most Chipewyan men take on the subject of bogeymen and, like Wellington, said "I never seen one." It was a more difficult situation for my wife. Only recently had she been exposed to horror movies, monsters, Halloween, and all the other undercurrents of magic in our modern society (O'Keefe 1983) and the past year in Vancouver

had added to her own lack of certainty. Bigfoot is very much a part of
the popular culture of the Vancouver area, and there had been a few
well-publicized sightings before we came north. We were all spending most of our time inside the camp, so my reactions and those of
my family became part of the information that was floating around
about *bekaycho*.

Wellington continued to guide for Corky and his wife, and they
killed a moose on the eleventh. The anxiety they felt about bears
and the wilderness was enhanced by an encounter with a barren
ground grizzly. The men saw the bear, took the boat to shore, and
got out to shoot it. The bear promptly charged them. Both Corky
and Wellington decided that retreat was the better part of valor,
Wellington later commenting about looking at those legs, "the size
of tree stumps," coming over the muskeg at him. The bear got away
unmolested, but the incident did not diminish the stories of strange
beasties out in the bush.

While Wellington was out guiding, George spent his time working around our camp. The conversations I had with him were often
about things we regard as supernatural, but he was also pondering
his and his wife's position in the camp. He had not abandoned the
idea that Wellington would gain control of the fish camp, telling me
on June 9, that he would move to Foxholm Lake in two weeks if con-
firmation did not come through. He indicated an awareness of his
wife's predicament and did say that she was a bit stingy. We talked
about the history of his marriage, and he said he did not mind her
now, going so far as to proudly state that he "had not hit her in two
years." This was not an admission of wife beating, for he was not a
wife beater, nor was Joan someone inclined to be beaten, but an idi-
omatic expression of the fact that they had not had a serious argument for some time. Still, George was not now a happy man, a dramatic change from his normal disposition.

On June 12, a plane arrived bringing Jean, Wellington's mother- in-
law,[4] and Miley, the eldest of her sons. They planned to spend the
summer with us. Wellington was hoping they would spend the fall
along with Paul and May, George and Joan, and me and my family.
Jean brought news that Paul and May were due back on the four-
teenth, and that they would have their second eldest daughter
Virginia's young son with them. This child was to stay here while

his mother went outside to attend courses relating to her job as a native teacher in the school. Virginia and her husband were to join us later for three weeks of vacation and caribou hunting.

Miley and his mother set their tent just south of Wellington's. The arrangement of the tents expressed the social relationships within the camp quite well. The gap between Wellington's tent and his mother-in-law's tent was slightly less than the gap between George's tent and mine. When Virginia came later in the summer, her tent was placed behind Paul and May's. Paul and May's tent was in line behind Wellington's, the two tents forming the social center of the camp.

George and Joan were told their son had been sent to the hospital at Minetown and would not return with Paul and May. Joan decided to go back to be with him, for his condition sounded serious. She would make the trip in the plane that brought back Paul and May. George felt that boarding outpatients for the hospital in Minetown was a lucrative operation. He complained that the medical authorities often prolonged the stay of children sent in from the bush, as it was cheaper for the government to board them in Minetown than to pay for a charter aircraft to return them to their parents. Medical care was one of the treaty obligations assumed by the Canadian government when it took title to Chipewyan land, but its delivery was not immune to budgets or bureaucratic cost cutting. The concept of adequate medical care has developed from last century's annual pass through the region of someone designated as medically qualified into modern, complete medical care. The ideal is neither achieved nor approximated in spite of the sometimes Herculean efforts of the provincial public health nurses.

Wellington's circumstances were changing rapidly. Corky decided that the fishing at South Lake was not up to the standard he expected, and he was going to fly south for his second week's fishing. Wellington was to go along and guide for him. Before they left, Corky agreed to finance a fish camp for Wellington on a nearby lake where the fishing was known to be good. There was some confusion as to just what was intended. Corky wanted a private cabin for his own fishing, while Wellington wanted a way to make a living. The proposed camp would have to meet both sets of requirements.

George wanted to use the fish camp's boat to bring in the meat from the moose Corky and Wellington had killed the day before, but as Wellington prepared to depart on June 12, he told George that he was not to use the boat and motor for any reason. This was a curious provocation. George was as skilled as Wellington and at least as responsible. Wellington's move offended Jean as well, as she and George had intended to split the meat with most of it going to her so she could make dry meat.

June 14 saw one of the rarities of the Indian north—the plane came when it was supposed to. Prearranged flights to bring Indian parties out of the bush are put at the bottom of the charter companies' dispatching priorities. The people generally have no other way to get out, and the companies give precedence to walk-in business, especially that from transient whites. Local folklore (of both pilots and Indians) has it that transient parties of whites, who had no kin around to ask after them, have been taken out into the bush and completely forgotten. One group was left there for more than three months before they were able to contact a passing plane from another settlement and arrange a flight out.[5] Paul and May had George's baby with them, so Joan, packed and ready to go, did not have to leave. They also brought Virginia's child, as we had heard, as well as their youngest son, Phil. They brought up the supplies people had ordered, so we were now set for awhile.

The following ten days were very quiet. The contact with the outside had brought with it the latest infections and everyone got sick. During the catching up on the latest news and gossip, there was ample opportunity to tell and retell the Bigfoot stories without Wellington's presence to restrain their content. Little Ann was so impressed by the stories that within ten days she saw two *bekaycho* near camp. She was always seeing bogeymen, so no one was particularly concerned, but each location where she said she had seen one was examined. No tracks were found, and the people figured she had just seen an animal or imagined the sightings. The children took *bekaycho* more seriously than did the adults; to them it did sound a lot like a bogeyman.

By June 15, both Paul and George had decided to move to Foxholm Lake as soon as possible, but their decision implied no immediate action. Wellington was gone, and Paul and May had to remain here until Virginia came for her child; they were unlikely to miss the chance to visit with her and her husband. Eleven people were now down with various colds or other infections, hence moving anywhere was beyond us for the moment.

The subarctic summer can be trying and does have its hot periods. Three weeks ago the lakes were ice water but Wellington's thermometer now hit 86° F in direct sunlight. In July it would reach 100° F. With the heat came the insects in full force. The small children had to be covered from head to foot, and the only way to do that was to dress them in winter clothing. Not a great deal could be done to avoid the insects except to stay inside the tents. Paul and Jean were the only ones who seemed to be content. Before the ice had gone bad, Paul had brought the remnants of an old canoe over from the cabins and was now happily rebuilding it. Jean was cheerfully helping May with the hide of the moose that Wellington had killed. The older generation of Chipewyan have to have work while they are in the bush. If they do not have enough to keep them busy, they become bored and then irritated, which leads to conflict. Jean was an extreme case, so much so that she would ask people to let her do their laundry just to keep herself busy.

I had arranged to have a canoe and motor sent up and they had duly arrived, but the motor malfunctioned and had to be sent back out for repair. The only other transportation was the boat and motor from the fish camp. Miley had taken to using it. He, Phil, and George took it out sometimes, but George usually stayed home. Miley's willingness to use the boat and motor were of no help in retrieving the moose meat. George said that it had gone bad by now, and even if it had been useable, he had no intention of helping bring it in after Wellington's departing insult. Miley was unwilling to try to find it from second-hand verbal directions, so the meat was lost.

The conflict between George and Wellington was in suspension while Wellington was gone. The tenor of the camp changed from anxiety and stress to lassitude marred only by irritation with the heat and the insects.

There are a variety of ways to interpret a figure like *bekaycho* in and of itself (MacNeish 1954; Needham 1978, 1980; Kenny 1981, 1982; Levi-

Strauss 1967; Beidelman 1961, 1963, 1971) but I am here less interested
in the figure than in the specifics of its social context. Utilization of
European mythical and quasi-mythical figures such as Cain and Abel,
the wild man, or wolf children might be helpful, but their use runs
too great a risk of obscuring the relevant social nuances through the
introduction of implicit Western cultural elements that are lacking
from the Chipewyan form. The Mission Chipewyan had no belief in
the Bigfoot, and I know of no exposure to the figure prior to 1975, but
the widespread Northern Athapaskan figure of the bushman is somewhat similar in form.

Anthropological interpretation of the bushman is scanty.
MacNeish (1954) and Slobodin (1960) provide the classic work on the
subject, but the general pattern of interpretation has followed that
set by Osgood (1933). Osgood drew upon earlier nonanthropological
traditions (Basso 1978:691; Van Stone 1965:105) in accepting fear as a
major factor in the bushman belief and identified the salient set of
characteristics. "The *Nakani* to them is a human being, generally an
Indian, who had taken on certain supernatural qualities. . . . Thus is
seen in the *Nakani* the purposes of killing men and stealing women
joined with the characteristics of superhuman strength, ability to go
unusual lengths of time without food, and an association with summer and the idea of the 'unseen' ". (Osgood 1933:85–86).

The characteristics of the bushman reported in the literature form
a recognizable set but vary substantially from place to place and time
to time. "According to the Hare, 'bushmen' are anthropomorphic
beings who roam around in the bush during the summer and steal
women and children. [Of human origin,] these days bushmen are only
white people." (Hara 1980:141). James Van Stone (1965:105) reports that
for the Snowdrift Chipewyan, "It is clear that 'bush men' are not
endowed with real supernatural powers, yet their shadowy existence
in the bush and their ability to live apart from other people make
them different from ordinary human beings." Van Stone refers to them
as "quasi-supernatural beings."

Robert Lowie (1925:325–365), among others, has reported the Windigo
figure among the Chipewyan, but just as bushmen must be differentiated from European forms to prevent the intrusion of alien elements
not existing in the data, so must this well-known cannibal monster
be differentiated from the bushman. I fear the attention given the

Windigo figure as found among neighboring Cree and more southerly boreal forest peoples has falsely informed analysis of the Athapaskans via an implicit assumption that the bushman is no more than a borrowed and weaker version of the Windigo; a version that fits the explanatory paradigms developed for those alien cultures. This may be the reason the bushman has attracted so little attention from Northern Athapaskanists.

The predominant mode of explanation has seen the bushman as a projective device expressing fear and anxiety, but two recent works have taken analysis of the figure in more profitable directions. Robert Jarvenpa (1977:165–183) has examined the motif along the upper Churchill River drainage, the terminus of southern expansion of the Chipewyan. He carefully restricts his analysis to a specific historical period, the 1930s, when there was a large influx of white trappers. His precision enables him to demonstrate that the motif then acquired, and has since held, a particular form, "depression era trappers." Jarvenpa's work contextualizes changes in the form, linking it irretrievably to the ongoing Chipewyan process of intellectual and emotional interpretation of culture change. Ellen Basso (1978:690–709) has argued, "a more fruitful approach is one that would examine their contexts of use as cultural symbols. In particular, because they seem often to be associated with descriptions of dangerous or even disastrous situations, it may be that they are embedded in broader notions of causality, and that the speech acts in which they appear can be taken to contain causal explanations of such situations" (p. 691). Both Basso and Jarvenpa recognize (and document) two significant features of the bushman that must guide the more properly sociological analysis advanced here: (1) the bushman motif is a changing form responding to particular historic circumstances and (2) bushmen are real entities sometimes found in the Canadian north.

The Mission Chipewyan use the term "boogeyman," more accurately bogeyman, in English and I will follow the second usage here. There are various kinds of bogeymen, each having some of a cluster of features. The most consistent of these are: living apart in the bush, wearing hard soled shoes, lurking around *dene* habitations, malicious temperament, theft, and a propensity for stealing people. This "cluster" of features is exactly that, a cluster.[6] Not all bogeymen have all of these attributes, but bogeymen are generally human, generally male, and generally adult.

The simplest form of bogeyman is the *Amoo*, a projected threat as a consequence of misbehavior that is used to regulate the behavior of young children and instill adherence to the authority of seniors. Adults do not accept their existence, at least I never heard of or met any adult who did so. Children sometimes holler *amoo! amoo!* to scare still younger children. There is a relativity in the usage of this form, the child scaring a younger child may in turn be scared by an adult. As children reach the borderline of acceptance of the form's reality, attempts to scare them with it may produce both anger and fear. I have seen small boys initially react with fear only to then become angry when they realized what had happened and how they had reacted.

Bogeymen of concern to adults fall into the general category of *udzena dene*, roughly "unpredictable person," or *ene dene*, thief person or enemy (Cree) person. As an ongoing and developing form, the bogeyman rapidly spins off new variants as circumstances change. There is, for example, a troglodyte form know as "dwarves" that is associated with the shaft of an abandoned uranium mine near Mission. Another type, "Germans," owes its current form to the expression of Franco-German political history through the dominance of French speakers among the oblate Missionaries. The first long-term resident priest in the area served in the French resistance during World War II and spoke often of his experiences.[7] This form of bogeyman ties directly to the mythical nature of World War II and Chipewyan perceptions of time. To them, in the early 1970s, that war was not over but was instead a reality of myth time raging continuously somewhere in the outside world.

Not all bogeymen are white, not all are male, and not all are human. In the material I gathered in 1970, there were two recent but separate encounters that involved the killing of six bogeymen. The first killing involved two Cree men and a red-haired white woman who were living together in the bush, well to the south of the village. The other killing involved three small, black, hairy males first thought to be bear by the young man who shot them just off the opposite shore of Mission Lake across from the village. This last case was the only one in which there was an attribution of excessive body hair to the bogeyman. These creatures were not gigantic or smelly, common attributes of the Sasquatch, or Bigfoot, and there was no mention of foot size. The accounts the people give of this particular incident say that the Royal Canadian Mounted Police (RCMP) constable and the priest went to the lake to look at the bodies. They buried them on the spot in unhallowed ground, and an unofficial silence descended over the event, as they have never spoken about what they had seen. This was interpreted by the local Chipewyan as proof that the bodies were neither human or bear.

In the summer of 1984, Mission was troubled by a series of bogeymen. Several men, apparently survivalists or members of a paramilitary organization, spent two weeks living in the bush in the vicinity of the village. They wore black fabric jumpsuitlike garments, likened by the local Chipewyan to skindiver's wet suits, complete with military webbing and attached pouches, survival gear (including large switch-blade knives) and token camouflage. They were not very adept at avoiding contact and were seen many times by residents of Mission (including Virginia and her husband) along the roads near the village and in the surrounding bush. These people engaged in no hostile activity but they refused to answer when they were spoken to. The Chipewyan always addressed them and offered assistance when they were seen, but the men always silently withdrew into the bush. Before the two weeks were up, they had so thoroughly established themselves as bogeymen that several times Chipewyan men fired upon them when they did not respond to being hailed.

Since 1975, these Chipewyan have been increasingly exposed to the symbolic and visual culture of the larger Canadian society. In addition to their own increased travel and a greater level of fluency in English, they have received television and local radio. The subsidized rental of high-frequency radio sets capable even of patching bush parties into the telephone system has removed much of the isolation of bush life. This modern technology gave one bogeyman sighting an entertainment value that was not possible in the past.

During the hunting and trapping season of 1977, a man[8] with the reputation for frequently seeing bogeymen got onto the radio at his isolated camp to tell of seeing a pair of bogeymen occupy his absent brother's adjacent empty cabin. His radio call reached back to the village and to the small administrative center a few miles to the west

and could be received by anyone listening in on his frequency. He
was terrified of the bogeymen's presence and continually sent pleas
for help over the radio. Word spread of his transmissions and more
and more people tuned into his fearful descriptions of the bogeymen's
actions and his own responses. He held the two settlements spell-
bound, one man I knew later said that listening in on the radio call
was "just like a movie." As the night drew on the isolated camper
became so terrified of the bogeymen that he would not even open his
door to get the firewood that was stacked outside. He burned the furnishings of his cabin to keep warm. Shortly after dawn two rescue
aircraft arrived. One was from the village and the other was an RCMP
aircraft from Yellowknife, hundreds of miles away. The RCMP, weapons ready, investigated the cabin reportedly occupied by the bogeyman and found an old boot to be its sole occupant. Never ones to let
a good story die, the Chipewyan gleefully informed me that the
Yellowknife RCMP had billed the village band for the cost of their
flight. How a man handles the bogeyman motif is related to his status in the community, not as a thing by which he gains it but as
something by which he can lose it.

If we find human bogeymen problematic, the nonhuman ones are
even more so. The human–nonhuman distinction is not marked by
the Chipewyan and they do not discriminate between them. Some
forms of bogeymen are featured in stories and myths surrounding
the "Magic Boy," a prophet of the early 1970s who was the reincarnation of a culture hero. He had, in a previous incarnation, killed some
bogeymen along a river near where Mission came to be. Their ghosts
still waited there for his return, to take vengeance upon him. In these
stories bogeymen are present before the Chipewyan language emerged,
thus if the form does not predate Western contact, it has been fed
into stories about events that do predate contact.

Children's reactions to bogeymen are more consistent than are
those of adults, but there is a rough parallel between them. Men say
that more women than men see or fear bogeymen and that corresponds to the behavior I observed, but male attribution is a rather
different phenomenon than observed female behavior and statements.
Men who see or fear or were reputed to see or fear bogeymen were
well known, as were women who professed not to fear or not to have

seen them. That this aspect of their behavior is important enough to be widely known is not likely to be without significance.[9]

I had few opportunities to observe how people reacted to bogeymen except among those people I knew well enough to camp with. Young women in their teens to early twenties see most of the bogeymen reported to enter the village, but most of the stories I have heard were told by women in their middle years and boys in their midteens. Almost all the adult women I knew had stories about some event in the bush that represented a bogeyman or bogeymen trying to harass them. Most older women had spent much of their adult life in the bush and had stories to tell about unseen bogeymen coming near them while the men were making long portages with equipment and supplies. Accounts of bogeyman behavior include throwing pebbles at the women and children while they waited for the men to return or skulking around in the bush just out of sight. I found no evidence to support the idea that it was men of their own party teasing or harassing them.

All bogeymen are dangerous. They have been known to murder and they have stolen women, children, and infants who were never seen again. Bogeymen are less of a threat to men, probably because Chipewyan men almost always go armed in the bush, whereas Chipewyan women are generally unarmed or only poorly armed.[10] Bogeymen will attack an unwary man if he is unguarded in his behavior or otherwise vulnerable. Bogeymen are often detected by dogs before people know they are around. Men traveling alone sometimes tie their dogs to the tent poles, making a wall of dogs around them to keep away bears, bogeymen, or whatever else might be wandering around out in the bush. This is not unreasonable. Wellington does not do this and twice in five years has had to kill a black bear tearing through his tent wall while he was inside sleeping. Some men have given me this reason in explanation for encouraging their dog teams to attack strangers without warning.

Whatever the actual distribution of "belief" (Needham 1972) in bogeymen, there are contexts in which all Chipewyan act as if bogeymen are real. Even people I knew not to believe in them would sometimes act this way. Location is also a factor in the beliefs. In 1970, when I was first asking about bogeymen, I asked Wellington, George, and

Fred (separately and on several occasions) if there were bogeymen at Foxholm Lake. Wellington simply said, "No." Fred explained that there were none up here and then proceeded to tell me stories about how his aunt had seen them even farther north. He finally launched into a lengthy explanation of how some people saw them and believed and some did not, giving names and events, before finally saying he had "never seen one." George graphically said, "No way, it's too fucking cold up this far."

The bogeyman is a recognized category for explaining certain types of events. In some of these cases it serves as a public explanation for very private events, a social fiction that requires a public expression of acceptance of the ability of the creatures designated by the category to cause certain kinds of events to happen. For a social fiction to be effective it is imperative that a significant portion of the population recognize that it is a fiction.

The most conspicuous use of bogeymen is as an explanation for what are probably accounts of murder, theft, death, infanticide, or other forms of violence. Older people, adults of the birth cohort first active in the 1930s and early 1940s, know of small children, usually the newborn or those too young to have ever been brought into a settlement, who were stolen by bogeymen and whose bodies were never recovered. These cases, whether of natural death, accident, or infanticide, are cover stories partly designed to put off investigation by the Canadian authorities.[11] These stories probably worked until the RCMP had ready access to float- or ski-equipped aircraft. The areas the Chipewyan trap and hunt are so vast and remote that a bogeyman story surfacing months after the event would have been unlikely to have prompted a police officer to journey hundreds of miles only to then have to search thousands of square miles of bush for the remains of a baby that no white person had ever seen. There may be a link between the stories and later bureaucratic requirements for the disposition of the body of a person who has died in the bush. Today, when a death occurs in the bush, the requirement to bring in the body to determine the cause of death means a lost season and expenses of hundreds, if not thousands, of dollars.

In a similar manner, bogeyman stories once functioned as an explanation for reporting alien Indian or Inuit boats, found curiously abandoned with their goods, whose owner obviously fell victim to a passing bogeyman. Could any policeman justify spending weeks going hundreds of miles into another governmental jurisdiction (the Northwest Territories) because he had heard in the spring that such a canoe had been found the previous summer if no one from the local community was missing and there was no evidence other than gossip? These stories are not current, not with the RCMP only a few hours' flight away. Neglect has long since replaced infanticide, and the adoption hunger in the south takes any unwanted baby the community can produce and others besides.

Bogeyman stories are still used to cover events best kept from the white man's attention. Wife-beating, child abuse, most of the things that can happen with the inappropriate expression of violence can be covered, at least for a time, if they happen in the bush where blame can be placed upon a bogeyman. When this happens, the adults of the community know exactly what has occurred. The victims do not refrain from telling their friends, kin, and peers, so the word spreads among the adults in the village. People maintain the social fiction that a bogeyman was at fault and comment how lucky they were to get the victim back from the bogeyman.[12]

A powerful aspect of the social fiction formed from stories of the bogeyman is the generation of a mechanism for male control of women and children.[13] If we assume, for the moment, that there is no such beastie as the bogeyman, then the targeting of women and children as its potential victims is significant. The substantial number of women who do not fear bogeymen does not negate this interpretation. The fact is that Mission Chipewyan women do not spend much time in the bush. When they do go, they go in groups and tend to have an armed male along with them. Life in this vast environment with its small population does not allow strict adherence to this as if it were an unbreakable rule, and women must sometimes go into the bush alone, but they do so hesitantly, as infrequently as possible, and never very far. Bogeymen even constrain the movement of women within the village. In the summer of 1970 I gathered about eighteen reported sightings inside the village in the course of a month.

All were at night and all were seen by women in their late teens or early twenties, the age group of the unmarried female population. My information on the number of sightings during that period is almost certainly incomplete. The bogeyman is an effective constraint upon women's freedom of movement, a constraint greater than what I sense from the literature to be the case for women in other Northern Athapaskan cultures.

Phil Moore, a former student, in the course of an investigation of the Salem witch trials, recognized that in the early accounts there was an elegant folk model that best resolved the sociological issues. The most parsimonious, if imperfect, solution to the question of why there were witch trials at Salem is to recognize the truth in native explanation. The witch trials began because there were witches; they ended because the authorities killed all of them. A major reason the Chipewyan have a bogeyman figure is because there are bogeymen.

To recognize that bogeymen exist as a rare but real feature of their environment is one thing, but how can this group of Chipewyan accept the existence of *bekaycho*—a creature of whom they had no previous knowledge and for whom they have no physical evidence?

The issue of belief has taken on new theoretical relevance in anthropology since the publication of Rodney Needham's *Belief, Language, and Experience* in 1972. In this work Needham addresses "Wittgenstein's question: 'Is belief an experience?'" Starting from this question, he examines our culture's category, "belief," and in a complex argument I will not summarize here, demonstrates that belief, "does not exist as a discriminable mode of consciousness." The import of Needham's work is that belief is a cultural construct and cannot be assumed to be an aspect of other cultures.[14] "Ordinary discourse and the common-sense psychology that is in part its product tend to induce us into two capital errors: first, the assumption that there must be something in common to all instances of believing; second, the assumption that there must be a mental counterpart to the expression of belief" (p. 122).

Several times in the present work, particularly with the atemporality of *inkoze* and the lack of resolution in explanation of events (e.g., the waterspout) we have had to confront the fact that the difference between Chipewyan categorization and our own, leads them to behavior not intuitively understandable to us. Formally, the question of Chipewyan belief in *bekaycho* is invalid, as it has not been demonstrated that the Chipewyan believe. Yet, the concept of belief is so crucial to our own understanding that it is necessary to show how the concept confounds our understanding of the Chipewyan, otherwise some of their actions will remain inexplicable.

Levy-Bruhl (1967, 1979) has argued that accepting the primacy of causality in terms of natural phenomenon is a cultural decision, one our culture has made. To accept the reality or existence of any phenomenon not demonstrable as a natural phenomenon is a matter of belief. The Bigfoot is a creature for whom no adequate natural evidence exists, hence acceptance of its existence is a matter of belief.

When our culture considers the Chipewyan category, bogeyman, it demands that we interpret the Chipewyan category in the same terms. Bogeymen fall into two types, human and nonhuman, since bogeymen cannot be animals. Any judgment as to the presence of a bogeyman must fall within one of the following possibilities: (1) bogeymen are nonhumans correctly perceived to be present, (2) bogeymen are nonhumans incorrectly perceived to be present, (3) bogeymen are humans correctly perceived to be present, or (4) bogeymen are humans incorrectly perceived to be present.

In Western terms, the nonhuman forms (1 and 2) are impossible by definition, so their existence is a question of belief. The human forms (3 and 4) can exist and be out there, their presence being a matter of a correct judgment upon the evidence in a particular situation (Figure 1).

FIGURE 1

The presence of belief in a Western Interpretation of Bogeymen.

|                       | Human | Non-human |
|-----------------------|-------|-----------|
| Correctly Perceived   | o     | +         |
| Incorrectly Perceived | +     | +         |

The Chipewyan combination of human and nonhuman forms within a single category generates an ambiguity in our interpretation of their actions in response to the category. The relevant factor in our understanding of their actions is either their accuracy in perceiving the situation or the issue of their belief in a form that to us is impossible.[15] As long as we impose the latter question upon the Chipewyan we will be incapable of understanding their actions. The multiple distinctions made in a Western interpretation of the Chipewyan forms create a false understanding of both the Chipewyan forms and their response to bogeymen and *bekaycho*. Chipewyan culture does not presume explanation in terms of natural phenomenon as the only valid form of explanation. The Chipewyan do not distinguish between human and nonhuman bogeymen or *bekaycho*; a bogeyman is a bogeyman, its humanity is irrelevant. The Chipewyan category collapses the distinctions we make, thus the question of belief is irrelevant. The only issue to them is the evidence about the presence or absence of the creature in any particular set of circumstances (Figure 2).

The stereotypical response of a Chipewyan man to bogeymen, "I never seen one" is not a statement of belief or disbelief in the existence of bogeymen, it is an exact statement of his observations that also expresses the adult male's perceived lesser vulnerability to bogeymen. When Chipewyan women and children react with fear and modify their behavior in light of their understanding of bogeymen, they are expressing their perceived greater vulnerability to bogeymen. Chipewyan men and Chipewyan women do not disagree about the existence of bogeymen but about their natural history. Men stereo-

FIGURE 2

Chipewyan Bogeymen/*bekaycho*

| | |
|---|---|
| Correctly Perceived | Human + Non-human |
| Incorrectly Perceived | Human + Non-human |

typically regard bogeymen as so rare as to not be worth worrying about. Chipewyan women stereotypically do not regard bogeymen as so rare as to not be worth worrying about.

There is, underlying this issue, another set of concerns that focuses upon the rationality of the Chipewyan and the role that rationality plays in our own symbolic ordering of culture, behavior, and thought. In essence the question is, how can the Chipewyan be rational beings if they accept that these illusory beings exist? As with the question of belief, the answer lies not in the Chipewyan but in the recognition that rationality—and its assumption of a hierarchical order of basic laws of thought— is a Western cultural creation. Rationality is not a condition of human existence supported by an unquestionable body of empirical data, but a cultural presupposition about the operation of the universe, the nature of human nature, and the operation of the human mind. In order to understand the actions of these Chipewyan, it will be necessary to escape this cultural trap of our creation and recognize that one of our most cherished philosophical assumptions "the law of noncontradiction (A is not not-A; contradictory judgments cannot both be true)" (Hobart 1985:115), is groundless and empirically false.

My earlier assumption about Chipewyan exposure to the Bigfoot before 1975 is questionable. This small group is but part of a larger local Indian population than nearing 650 people that has been constantly exposed to English- and French-speaking Canadian culture and to a yearly influx of American culture in the form of tourist fishermen. The probability of their not having been exposed to Bigfoot before 1975 is slight. The safest assumption is that the larger population had been exposed to Bigfoot but that the motif had not taken. If the people in the smaller group had been exposed to the Bigfoot before Corky's arrival, they had discarded it as without meaning.

Even in my best fieldwork form I was unable to insert myself into that boat along with Corky and his wife who were paying a small fortune for some quiet fishing on their vacation.[16] I would hazard a guess that the Bigfoot stories did not take up a great deal of their time and that Corky's wife was the odd person out. At least part of the telling of the stories must have been due to Corky's teasing her about her fears of the wilderness in order to hide his own fears. The genesis of these stories seemed to lie in this anxiety they shared about their nightly isolation at the fish camp. Some of this anxiety had to be communicated to Wellington, giving the stories a significance they might not otherwise have had.[17]

The relationship between Corky and Wellington partly explains why Wellington told us the stories. Tourist fishermen are always telling stories to their guides as well as expounding upon politics, work, life styles, and the meaning of life. Few of these monologues go far beyond the boat and fewer yet are understood by the guide. Had it been a fisherman other than Corky I doubt if the stories would even have been told back at our camp, although I do not wish completely to exclude the possibility that the Bigfoot stories were inherently interesting. However, Corky's influence extended only to Wellington. The relationship between these two men was a carefully constructed peer relationship rather than a hierarchical one, and Corky's role as an authority figure back at the camp was nonexistent. Neither did Wellington exercise sufficient authority for the other people in the camp to accept the stories just because he was the one to tell them.

Wellington's command of English was also a factor. For a man in his position, who earned cash by working with and for English speakers, English was a tool that could make the difference between an income and no income. The proficiency with which it is used often determines success or failure in job hunting and job performance. Language is also something heavily bound by context and situation and the illusion of proficiency can be created by staying within particular situational contexts. Wellington was capable of using English to perform as a guide and carry on conversations relating to subjects he knew well, such as hunting, trapping, or animal life, but he was lost as soon as a conversation moved into an area with which he had no personal experience. His understanding of the stories Corky told him about Bigfoot was rudimentary.

Wellington, who in two previous periods of fieldwork I had been unable to get to comment on the bogeyman as other than a joke, did not come back to camp a converted believer but as the bearer of curious stories his friend had told him. To retell the stories, Wellington had to perform an immediate reinterpretation of them into a form he was used to, one that fit his own cultural matrix and that of his listeners. Wellington had no small skill at manipulating verbal forms and by the time he retold them in camp, even though they were attributed to Corky, they were systematically reformed versions of the Chipewyan bogeyman stories with which Wellington was familiar. What diffused between the two cultures was not Bigfoot but *bekaycho*, a hithertofore unknown bogeyman that carried a translation of Bigfoot's name. The motif of one culture, Bigfoot, provided a stimulus for the creation of a new form, *bekaycho*, in another culture—one similar to, but independent of, the original stimulus.

A constant feature of Bigfoot once it was transformed into *bekaycho*, was its association with social relationships undergoing redefinition. The camp was not its old self and never again would be its old self. George turned to the supernatural when faced with events that placed his own social position in jeopardy. Paul displayed a similar reaction when faced with the dead fox and his son's streak of bad luck caribou hunting. Wellington himself was under stress, for his position was also changing. George and Wellington were only a part of the group and their relationship to each other only part of their relationships to others in the camp. They did not cease to be husbands, sons, fathers, or brothers-in-law just because they were changing the way they related as brothers; they did not cease to hunt, fish, chop wood, feed the dogs, scratch insect bites, sleep, eat, or a thousand other things because this one relationship was changing. In the welter of other roles and statuses they occupied, the change was a minor thing. Even the status of changing a relationship was not unique to them. Little Ann was changing from prepubescent female to young adult; only six or seven years away from motherhood and marriage. Mike was changing from small child to large child with very real differences in responsibilities and privileges. Miley was about to become wealthy. Paul was weakening at a discernible rate and his whole social position was changing. Jean was on the verge of becoming an old woman incapable of the physical activities she has performed all her adult life.

In a small group so thoroughly mixed by age and gender there was constant change as each person moved through the life cycle. The camp that I said a few lines ago was not its old self, never was its old self. The scale of social life is too small for the stability and lack of change we choose to believe are features of life in our own larger

society to be a feature of Chipewyan life. There are so few players
and each individual plays so many roles that interlock with those of
the same other players, that each player becomes almost larger than
life and almost every role includes constant change as one of its features. In this constant change and redefinition there is ample flexibility to adopt and apply a minor symbolic form.[18]

The role the men played in establishing *bekaycho* is significant
but secondary, even going so far as to assume an unconscious male
conspiracy to promote *bekaycho*. The women and children were the
ones with the crucial role in spreading the motif and maintaining it
for transmission into the future. Logic would seem to indicate that
they would balk at yet another threatening feature in their lives. All
the normal bogeyman features were already in place and there was
no discernible female revolt or assertion of independence that would
seem to call for or make useful the imposition of a new form. The
women's movements were constrained already by the presence of the
mosquitoes and black flies, the difficulty in walking very far over a
rather rough section of terrain, and of being nearly fifty air miles
from the nearest occupied camp. There was nowhere else for them
to go. It may be that if some bogeymen are an effective means of controlling the women then even more is better, but this ignores the
role of the women and children in defining *bekaycho* and making it
a viable feature of the culture of the camp.

Reactions to the bogeyman are a factor in basic individual concerns such as the perception of nature, self-identity, and sexuality,
but the men could only share in telling the stories and talk about
them. Acceptance of *bekaycho* had to be generated by the women
and children themselves. Recognizing that the reality of bogeymen
and *bekaycho* is not at issue for the Chipewyan ties together the specifics of its diffusion via the women and children and its role in male
control of them.[19] The actions of the women and children were a logical and rational response to a real but previously unknown threat.
Most importantly, why must a bogeyman be other than another
Chipewyan beyond the chance of observation or discovery? Where is
the line between foolishness and sound common-sense precautions,
and how many of our own precautions and beliefs involve categories
of persons no less rare than bogeymen? To ignore information like
this is to court peril and the ones most interested in it are the ones

most at risk. The spread of *bekaycho* to the Chipewyan was a sound precautionary move on the part of the women and children. Responding to the perceived vulnerability of their culturally generated age and gender roles, they themselves created a further means of male control over their persons as an unintended byproduct of their interest in their own self-preservation, while at the same time reaffirming the obligations of the male role toward them and further binding the males to them through the very assertion of their vulnerability and dependency.

Having completed the analysis of the women's reaction to *bekaycho* as a rational response to a potential threat, I cannot but caution that the very neatness and rationality of the explanation must serve to cast strong suspicion upon it. This work began by asserting that Chipewyan political behavior negated the assumptions of a utilitarian analysis. It further required the abandonment of the concept of belief as a prerequisite to understanding the figure of the bushman. In the light of Firth's (9185:29–46), Hobart's (1985:104–134), and Parkin's (1985:135– 151) devastating critiques of rationality, it is most unsatisfactory to leave the interpretation of these women's actions dependent upon that concept. Their response was self-generated rather than imposed and the men took their sightings seriously enough to investigate them, but it is not satisfactory to rely too heavily upon the real presence of bogeymen. A better approach is to be found in the relationship between reason and emotion in Western culture and in viewing ethnographic analysis as an aspect of that culture attempting to engage in cross-cultural interpretation.

Rationality in fact presupposes that reason and emotion are not in conflict but are shaped by each other and convince more through an apparent rightness of "feel" and "fit" than by any demonstrable proof (Parkin 1985:140). My initial analysis of the women's response to *bekaycho* has a certain appeal precisely because its aesthetics fit our own presuppositions about rational behavior in response to a threat and our assumptions of an integrated mind dominated by verbal cognitive processes. Neither justification of the analysis can face the reality of the data or the increasing physiological evidence that Western philosophical conceptualizations of the mind are incorrect.

The crucial element of an argument for the women's behavior as a rational response is the presence of fear and that is precisely the emotion that was lacking from their reactions. They were at times curious, skeptical, uncertain, and perhaps even anxious about *bekaycho* but there was no fear. The assertion of rationality proves dependent, not upon intellectual interpretation of their situation and responses, but upon our projection upon them of an affectual state. An affectual state that fits how we think they should feel with their beliefs in their situation; an affectual state they did not display. This situation well illustrates the interpretive problem (*see* Introduction). To argue that any human group responds in a nonrational manner is morally offensive within the context of our culture. Rationality is presumed to be the antithesis of an emotional response yet it proves to depend upon the presumption of an emotional state. Since the requisite emotion, fear, was lacking in the Chipewyan behavior, their behavior cannot be rational, yet to characterize it as nonrational is derogatory.

The first lesson these Chipewyan women have to teach is not at all about the Chipewyan but about the limits, and coercive power, of our own cultural categories and understandings. The issue is not whether or not Chipewyan behavior is rational, but the recognition that the concept is neither applicable nor capable of explaining their actions. The concept of rationality, a seeking of explanation in terms of modes of thought, is quintessentially — if deceptively — reductionistic. To escape this problem we must seek explanation at a more basic sociological level and recognize that these Chipewyan women are social beings engaged in a continuous process of negotiating their social status and gender roles. *Bekaycho* was a means by which their identity and status as females vis-à-vis the males was affirmed, and the particular obligations and duties of the males toward them were reasserted in changing circumstances.

1. I was not able to talk to Corky much after the first day, so I do not know the specifics of his beliefs. I have no reason to assume they differed from the common repertoire of American culture. Bigfoot should be taken to represent a more general name for the North American Sasquatch, the latter generally restricted to those sightings in the Pacific Northwest from northern California to British Columbia and southeastern Alaska. The distinction between Bigfoot and Sasquatch is not normally thought out among the populace at large. In the absence of material remains to resolve

the issue, it is best to assume that the difference between them is one of regional folklore that was beyond Corky's ken.

2. When Wellington had troubles with the Crown a few years later, Corky arranged for him to have the best possible legal services without ever considering their cost or seeking reimbursement.

3. Our camp was within rifle range. The prospect of the urban Corky firing upon phantoms of the night was a bit disconcerting.

4. Jean was Ann's mother, but she also stood in a number of different relationships to key people in the camp. She was a grandmother by relative age to all the children as well as grandmother by genealogical position to Wellington's children. She was an in-law to Paul and May. Paul and May's eldest daughter, not residing here, had married Jean's dead husband's brother's son some years before, establishing a diffuse cousin (*sela*) relationship with her. Such an overlap in relationships is common among the Chipewyan and may be a practical reason for their lack of interest in genealogies. Too great a recall of genealogical history might well make any useful discrimination between persons on the basis of kinship well nigh impossible. Affinal kinship is equally effective in creating functional social groupings and is not carried on generation after generation as is kinship through "descent."

5. The aircraft that had brought Jean was not making a split charter. She had to pay for her entire trip, whereas the cost of a complete charter was included in Corky's fees. Double charging is lucrative and a common practice.

6. Some other, but less constant, associations and features include: warm weather sightings, lack of grooming and unkempt appearance, secretive use of machinery, frightening dogs, excessive drinking, murder, and vindictiveness. I have no explicit evidence that bogeymen rape but that is implicit in many of their actions. Bogeymen reproduce, or at least have ancestors and will seek revenge for actions perpetrated upon their ancestors. Bogeymen are a category in Chipewyan culture, but not one marked by a single word. I suspect that one of the attractions of the English word bogeyman is that it unites the various forms by a single term.

7. Knowingly or not, the priest chose a powerful analogy to explain his actions in killing German soldiers. He equated the act with killing caribou, giving it resonances of meaning with Chipewyan myth in which certain powerful medicine men kill Cree as if they were caribou.

8. A troubled soul given to fits of alcoholic violence, he was probably drunk on homebrew at the time.

9. This information was gathered in English and the word "belief" was always used by informants and translators.

10. A more subtle gender role factor enters here. Even when Chipewyan women have immediate access to a weapon in a situation like this, using a weapon against a large, dangerous, and unseen creature is not their preferred response.

11. Infanticide is an emotionally charged topic subject to erratic definition. I regard serious neglect leading to malnutrition with its greatly increased probability of death from infectious disease as akin to infanticide. The deliberate killing of infants is attributed only to white trappers married to native wives save for one instance in which it was attributed to a local woman. That case was more a political metaphor concerning her husband than anything else.

12. Obviously there are limits to the effectiveness of the cover. It takes only one outraged person to involve the RCMP.

13. I am prepared to exclude extreme cases, such as the ones considered above, because wife-beating and child abuse move into other categories of real or potential violence that transcend the bogeyman as an analytical issue.

14. This issue is of particular import to investigation of primitive thought as an aspect of a more general turn to thought and the mind as a means of explanation. Levi-Strauss's (1981:625–695) passionate defense of the human mind as an explanatory device has been followed, perhaps inevitably, by a series of works by others focusing upon cognitive processes. In their extreme forms, they negate sociological explanation entirely and some even go so far as to reintroduce introspection as a form of evidence!

15. *Bekaycho*, in Western terms, is a simple category. All possible forms of the Bigfoot from which it is derived are matters of belief, so *bekaycho* can only be a matter of belief. Our cultural understanding of the Chipewyan form hinges upon the accuracy of our perception of the presence of humans in the environment; all other possibilities are questions of false belief.

16. Not that I didn't try.

17. If the origin of Bigfoot's transformation into *bekaycho* lies in the tourists' projection of their anxieties about isolation in a fearful and hostile environment with which they could not cope, then we have a delightful irony. This precise psychological argument has been advanced for the existence of both the Windigo and the bushman among Canadian subarctic peoples.

18. Needham's explication of polythetic classification may be useful here (1972, 1975, 1978).

19. Women and children fall into a single category here much as they did in relation to *inkoze*.

# Chapter Seven

Wellington was paid when Corky left at the end of the week and received a handsome cash tip and some expensive presents. Back at the base fish camp near Mission, he was given the wages due him and George for their repair of the outpost camp. Instead of returning to South Lake he made a charter flight to the liquor store in Minetown and spent the next week partying with friends. Wellington returned June 23 with most of the money he had earned spent on the parties and the charter aircraft. George became angry as he sorted through the small amount of fishing tackle Wellington had brought him. His worst fears about Wellington's intent to pay him fairly, if he had gotten ownership of the fish camp, seemed confirmed by what George took to be an appropriation of the wages he had earned cleaning the camp.

Chipewyan egalitarianism is expressed in many contexts far removed from what is normally thought of as the political. The ideology of siblingship establishes that a brother has the right to use, without seeking permission, anything that belongs to another brother. This is one of the leveling mechanisms that prevent the establishment of asymmetry and hierarchy through wealth and ownership. Some *dene* even include cash and paychecks within this ideological framework, while others assert under certain circumstances the right of sexual access to a brother's wife. This special relationship between brothers is recognized by animals in both their natural and supernatural aspects, as brothers are able to remove fur from each other's traps without the one who set the trap incurring the wrath of the trapped species. Dog teams that are made up of littermates are said not to fight with each other and to share other virtues because of their siblinghood and its concomitant coresidence. These ideals are not achieved in practice of course, and are rarely even asserted by brothers who have separated to establish their own households. However, to deny their applicability toward a particular brother is a not inconsequential challenge to the logic and meaning of that special relationship.

I fear that because of Wellington's stronger personality George may seem to be simply a victim of Wellington's actions. This is not the case, and that shows in this small conflict. Wellington may have, arguably, misused his brother's wages, but he did not own the fish camp. For George to fault Wellington for not fairly paying him, for work that he did not perform at a camp his brother did not own, is nothing more than George's projection of the changing definition of his relationship with Wellington.

After his partying, Wellington had not the funds to purchase milk for his infant daughter, and this brought reprobation toward both him and Ann from May and Jean. The lack of milk meant that the child had to be continued on a diet of the liquid drawn from boiled oatmeal supplemented by what powdered milk Ann could borrow. This was not just poor planning or budgeting but an expression of a deliberate neglect that would later result in the infant being removed from the custody of her parents.

Wellington's domestic life was strained if not outright painful. His economic aspirations had suffered a crushing blow with the loss of the fish camp; Corky's promise of another camp was yet but a promise and surely far in the future. His brothers-in-law were a disappointment, all they could think about was spending their inheritance. Even if Wellington never articulated or planned to gain influence over the affiliation of his father and brother, he was unable to avoid perceiving the collapse of his potential influence. I think Wellington was now simply marking time until the fall caribou migration, playing out in a half-hearted manner his role in the firmly scripted separation of his brother and father. He too would soon begin to seek a way to leave South Lake.

George's hostility toward his situation and his brother grew increasingly stronger. In spite of his anxiety about Wellington's bid to control the fish camp, its collapse removed George's own reasons for being on this lake. I took the plane that brought Wellington south and when I returned later that same day, George was dissatisfied with the purchases I had made for him as he had earlier been with the purchases Wellington had made. His ensuing outburst set off another series of arguments, the end result of which was Paul and May sitting irritably in their tent, Wellington lost within some impenetrable mood in his, and Joan and George in tears in their tent. As the arguments had bounced around, George and Joan had received harder than they gave. George was not skilled at disguising affect, and for the next few days he did not receive the support that he needed to offset his increasingly less logical presence here.

In a small camp the consequences of a burst of anger are immediate. May was the only person with a sufficient combination of structural position and sentimental ties such that everyone would accept her anger without responding. Outbursts of anger by other persons spread through the camp, in turn setting off further arguments and outbursts. Much of the self-control and suppression of emotion that the Chipewyan display, derives from their direct experience of the social consequences of not suppressing anger in situations like this. Holding a camp together in the isolation of the bush requires constant effort and management from everyone in full awareness of the potential consequences of failure. D. M. Smith (1985:73–77) has insightfully argued that a major component of Chipewyan myth and storytelling is consciously directed at precisely this issue. "They usually have a very straightforward meaning which is equally profound. Most of their myths reflect anxiety about getting enough to eat and counsel cooperation and respect for one another and for all living things."

There is always a conscious and deliberate aspect to Chipewyan social relations as people work to preserve and maintain their existing patterns of interaction, but to see people solely as conscious of their motivations, carefully thinking ahead and planning their actions, reduces the individual to a cold and rather sinister automaton. When Fortes and Evans-Pritchard (1940:1–23) made explicit that political symbols are also values, they resolved this difficulty by articulating the relationship between social forms, categories, and symbols. They provided a way to understand how individuals can respond in a coherent, logical, and patterned manner without conscious deliberation of their course of action.

Summer games are one thing, but come winter the Chipewyan cannot tolerate excessive sensitivity to the feelings and actions of others. Their quarters are cramped, the light is bad, the dark long, and the cold intense. Winter conditions are often harsh, unpleasant, and deadly. The Chipewyan are unable to afford our cultural games of fashionable neurosis and dependency. In a culture that is heavily egalitarian through the denial of any assertion of control over the self, much of what seems to be mere insensitivity is in fact a critical art that must be mastered under circumstances where collective nonfunctioning can be rapidly fatal, and the ability to carry a nonfunctioning individual is severely limited. The controlled insensitivity of Chipewyan egalitarianism does not eliminate the irritations, spites, and piqués that are an inevitable and integral part of human social life, but it is one way to keep everyone functional in spite of them.

The growing conflict and frustration between the two brothers climaxed in the course of a short trip the three of us made on June 25. In the last stages of the spring trip from Mission, as George and I came over from Stop Lake to South Lake, the wet snow stuck to the heavily laden toboggans. At George's suggestion, I had left a ten-gallon drum of gasoline where we could pick it up later. Gasoline for the outboard motors was now in short supply, and we decided to go and pick up the drum.

We towed my canoe behind the fish camp's motor boat to the north end of the lake where a portage had to be made around the rapids where we had seen the otter in the spring. We left the boat above the rapids and took the canoe and motor down the river toward where the gasoline had been left. Wellington was running the motor as we moved slowly down the river, George in the front and I again in the middle, this time facing backward. We came upon a cow moose and her calf standing on the south bank of the river watching us. Wellington quickly shut off the motor and turned the canoe so that it would drift in toward the shore where the moose stood. George and Wellington carefully took out their rifles and fired nearly simultaneously, killing the cow but not her calf. Both must have hit the cow, but I could not tell who fired the fatal shot. Wellington, I think, shot a fraction of a second earlier than George. He received credit for the kill; took credit for the kill. George was convinced he had hit the moose but was not yet prepared to argue down his brother; the same pattern that we have seen time and again.

The boat was quickly beached near the cow, and as soon as they confirmed she was dead, set off into a dense stand of trees in pursuit of the calf. They could not find it in the heavy brush so they tried to to flush it out by burning the stand of trees into which it had run. They assured me there was no risk of starting a forest fire as the stand was damp and surrounded entirely by open water muskeg. The fire failed to drive out the calf, so they returned to the cow and began to butcher her. They speculated about whether or not the calf was old enough to survive on its own but felt certain that through ignorance it would blunder into bear or wolves. My canoe was a small, fifteen foot sports model, already cramped with three of us in it, but it was such a calm and windless day that we overloaded it with the hide and as much of the most perishable meat as we could get in around us. The remainder of the cow was stacked and covered and we departed for camp, leaving the gasoline for another day.

We had only gone a few hundred feet, the water lapping within a few inches of the gunnels, when George began to discuss what he was going to do with the moosehide.[1] Wellington had the hide from the moose he and Corky had killed and Jean was already tanning it, so George felt he had an unquestionable claim to this one. His confident assertion of his right to the hide was soundly based in the ideology of shared hunting parties. He was along on the hunt, had seen the moose as soon as his brother, had shot at it and hit it. George needed the hide for moccasins and gloves, a need that a brother could hardly deny without creating an uncomfortable asymmetry of resources that would impinge upon George's ability to function in an effective manner come winter.

Wellington denied George's claim to the moosehide.[2] His position was unequivocal: he had killed the moose and it was his to do with as he saw fit. To add insult to injury, Wellington advanced in defense of his action another aspect of the sibling ideology, saying that he had promised the hide of the next moose he killed to a sister so that she could make herself a beaded jacket. Compared to George's estimate of his own need, this was a frivolous use of the hide. Once more George's lack of assertiveness and reliance on convention came face to face with his brother's aggressiveness, but this time he was not prepared to back down.

There followed a loud and nasty argument during which Wellington turned off the motor so he could give his full attention to the dispute. I was the only one watching the freeboard of the boat, giving it more attention than the argument, as we wallowed and drifted down the river. The argument shifted from the moosehide to money, from money to fishing gear and other goods, and then into a general set of accusations of stinginess and failure to live up to kinship obligations. Each aired his grievances in short but passionate bursts of verbalization. The argument stopped when Wellington shifted it to Joan's character and began to make harsh comments about her and her behavior. George ceased to respond and lapsed into a glowering and stony silence that lasted all the way through the trip upriver, the portaging of the canoe and meat, and the ride in the motorboat back to camp.

Before he started the motor to resume our trip up the river, Wellington, of all those in camp the person most concerned about keeping me informed, affirmed the seriousness of the argument by trying to explain what had been said in an English considerably less proficient than George's.

When we reached camp George stormed to his tent, abandoning the meat and his claim to it. Wellington beached the boat and deliberately walked to his own tent, informing everyone within hearing of the argument and his own position in the dispute. It was left to Miley and me to carry the meat up the hill. George refused the share of the meat that I brought to his tent. Competing versions of the argument made the rounds of the camp, polarizing everyone there and leading to a series of secondary arguments, including a nasty series of verbal exchanges between Wellington and Ann.

The argument put Paul and May on the spot and both of them had an immediate interest in seeing it resolved. May's concern was that of a mother's for fighting sons, and she wished to see peace returned to her family. Paul shared these concerns as their father but unlike May, he would have to choose between them if it did not end. For Paul to do nothing, to simply stay where he was, would be to side with Wellington, but to leave would be to side with George. Paul and May had arranged the marriage between George and Joan and they were forced to defend this unpopular woman. Joan was part of the idiom of the conflict, hence supporting her was de facto support for George and a defense of the legitimacy of their own actions as parents. They took the position that Wellington was wrong to have spoken to his brother the way he had done, but they were very low-key about the whole thing. I somehow doubt that conflict and argument between their children was something entirely new to them. The rights and wrongs of the disposal of the moosehide were quite thoroughly ignored by everyone but the sister to whom Wellington had promised it.

May occupied the position of sentimental authority and tried to quiet her sons by using their mutual tie to her. She had the weight of morality that came from being the one person least interested and best situated to define appropriate behavior. Paul did not intrude into this process nor did he try to use his structural legitimacy to intervene. He acted only to prevent any rash behavior. A precipitous departure by George would risk the healing of this breach and endanger the working arrangements developed through the years. The old canoe he had begun to rebuild gave him a measure of control over George, as none of the other boats were suitable for a cross-country move. Unless an unexpected aircraft were to arrive, and George could make arrangements to fly his family to Foxholm Lake on credit, that canoe would be the only way he could leave.

Anthropologists are enamored of the analysis of the form of the social groupings Northern Athapaskan peoples create to exploit their environment, but what a situation like this makes manifestly clear is that our commitment to those forms is greater than the commitment the people themselves have to them. These groupings are functional and necessary but they are not fixed or permanent. Even those that endure for years must be recreated each and every time the people move from a population concentration into isolation. What is of value to the people, beyond the immediate focus of the self and the conjugal family, is the unity and cohesiveness of the wider body of kin and affines from whom each actualized social grouping is drawn. It was to the significance and unity of this larger nonresidential group that Paul quickly turned, adopting a simple strategy: keep everyone in the same place and see if a resolution occurs. He continued his daily routine and did not seek opportunities to become involved in trying to resolve the conflict.

From the first negotiations over where we should go back in early April, there had been a geographical aspect to the expression of power in the interpersonal relations of these individuals. This single village of Chipewyan has a vast and nearly uninhabited field in excess of fifty thousand square miles upon which they can project their social relationships. They have few resources or material possessions that are not nearly uniformly distributed among them. What they do have and do control is their labor and their participation. Verbal representations of geographical placement and physical movement are more frequent than are actual physical expressions but verbally and physically, potentially and actually, geographical placement is a statement of participation and alliance; a metaphor for the expression of power.

The Chipewyan are keen observers of their environment and are acute natural historians. Their knowledge is of a very different order than that of Western ecology and biology but it is often more than the equal of the best science has to offer. Their way of knowledge encompasses not just knowledge of their environment but also includes knowledge of how their social system operates in that environment (Stanner 1963, 1964, 1965b). Natural historical knowledge is not the basis upon which they situate themselves in their land. They locate themselves upon the basis of the current state of their relationships and then utilize their natural historical knowledge of their environment to wrest their subsistence wherever they have chosen to go. The rhetoric they use to explain where they go sounds as if it is based upon natural history, particularly upon caribou behavior and ecology, but it is only rhetoric. Any attempt to understand how they utilize and relate to their environment by beginning with the physical environment rather than the social environment is ultimately doomed to failure.

Expressing power in metaphors of place is consonant with other mechanisms for, and the social dynamics of, the expression of power in interpersonal relationships. Chipewyan generally maneuver the actions of others indirectly, avoiding confrontation or attempts at direct control. The Chipewyan deal social position to social position rather than individual personality to individual personality, an avoidance of fixing the self, in accord with the passiveness of the actor paradigms in the conceptualization of causality in the culture. Direct expressions of power—individual personality to individual personality—among adults in conflict situations always have the inherent potentiality of a permanent termination of relations.

Before twenty-four hours had passed, in his first unilateral declaration of intent, George committed himself to moving away no matter what his father or I did. He said he was going to Foxholm Lake and was going to stay there for two years. He would not worry about resupply here but get interim supplies from EtΘen-che, the old wolf poisoner who lived with his aunt two lakes north of Foxholm Lake. Stating an intention is far removed from carrying it off, especially here where desire so rarely coincides with possibility, but a simple statement can be a powerful factor in ordering human relations. George's declaration, however far removed from immediate execution or unrealistic the figure of two years might be, made the separation of the group a fact rather than a threat. George did not really wish to make the trip to Foxholm Lake by canoe, as to do so would be very dangerous, but we did not expect any more planes until Virginia and her husband, Eddy, came up for their holidays. Paul kept on working at rebuilding the old canoe but did so at his own pace and made no promises of an early completion.

Wellington drifted off into himself, spending most of his time taking his wife and children on picnics in the fish camp's boat or going off with Miley. He displayed the same pattern of isolation in the midst of a social grouping that George and Joan had shown earlier, during the spring berry picking. His relations with his parents, in particular with May, were tense. She chose this time to castigate him for his treatment of his daughter, publicly placing upon him the moral onus that until now had been handled gingerly. Only Miley seemed indifferent to the situation.

This time the moose meat was not abandoned. Miley and I went out in the heat spell we were having and brought it in on June 27. After we had carried it all in we discovered that much of it had already gone bad. Neither Wellington or George wanted any of the meat. George refused all that I tried to give him and went so far as to stand in front of his tent and glower as Miley and I lugged it up the hill from the boat. Wellington gave all of his to Jean so she could make dry meat.

Surrounded by ill feelings, bored, and frustrated that his brother had killed two moose, George decided to try some moose hunting of his own. He took Miley out on June 28 and killed one. He wanted to give the entire hide to Miley (for Jean), but Joan balked and made him keep his half. Being so generous to Wellington's mother-in-law would have been an effective way to shame Wellington, if Joan had let him carry it off.

He went out alone the following day and killed another moose. Assuaged by these successes and with his separation from Wellington already determined, he tried to make peace with his brother on June 30, yielding to Wellington his claim to purchase my snowmobile. He said he felt bad about the fight with his brother. The weight of the kinship tie was working on him and he was seeking to reestablish relations on the basis of the new social arrangements. These overtures were made through third persons and were a sign of returning normalcy, but Wellington would have no part of them.[3]

On July 2, I attempted to get Wellington and George to go fishing with me. I made no secret that I was asking both of them. George refused outright and Wellington remained in his tent, saying the black flies were too bad.

The children remained more or less uninvolved in the dispute between the adults. George's daughter seemed a little more isolated than usual but that could just as easily have been due to the insects. Jean and Miley were able to deal with both George and Wellington and their families, but contact between George and Miley was limited. Jean and Joan discovered they got along well and enjoyed working together. In spite of the heat and insects, Jean was working outside. She simply could not abide inactivity. She had already completed the first stages of work on the hide from George and Miley's moose and was now behind George's tent helping Joan prepare the hide from the moose George had just killed. This was not just work but an opportunity to teach a person whose company she enjoyed. Joan's skill at preparing hides was limited. She had already ruined one hide earlier this spring and did not wish to ruin this one too. The two women had removed the hair from the hide and were scraping the inside to remove the debris and fatty tissue that can ruin the hide during tanning. It takes strength and skill to scrape the raw hide thoroughly enough to clean it without putting holes in it and reduce it to a uniform first approximation of the desired thickness of the finished leather. Everyone else was inside, but Ann happened to step out of her tent and saw the two women. She returned and told Wellington what they were doing. He was infuriated by his mother-in-law's actions. Coming out of his tent to see for himself what they were doing, he stood a moment and then yelled across the camp for Jean to get away from there and not help "that woman."

Jean was stunned. Wellington's treatment of her was insulting and disrupted something she genuinely enjoyed doing. She retreated in tears back across the camp, passing Wellington with her head down. She retired to her own tent and shortly afterward announced her intention to return to the village on the first available aircraft.

It is hard to know what to make of Wellington's action. Jean was an affine of a superior generation, old enough to be entitled to respect, and not even a dependent of his. Her husband's vanishing into the bureaucratic maze outside had left her independent for years, and she was one of the few women in the village to head a functional household. As a woman she was not caught in the men's webs of *inkoze* and was able to temporarily attach herself to other clusters of kin without losing her autonomy. She was simply not part of their game. Wellington had no moral basis for his action and it was a stunningly stupid move. Gender solidarity among the women now began to work against him. A number of women and older girls who had sided with him in his dispute because of their hostility toward Joan, now saw themselves threatened by his assertion of control over an independent woman's right of association. I am almost inclined to think of his action as deliberate, not an attempt to win the dispute with George, but a striking out in frustration to clear the stage and regain the isolation he also enjoyed.

The next several weeks were a bit of muddle for everyone, including me. The full heat of the summer was upon us and a severe lethargy descended upon the camp, caused in part because no one was certain of how to act toward anyone else in the camp. Everyone was waiting to see what would happen. George and Wellington largely avoided one another. After the development of open conflict between the brothers, *bekaycho* was not talked about, and I assumed it had been rejected as a viable addition to their culture. That this was not to be the case depended upon events that were then unknowable.

George continued his moose hunting binge, killing another one on July 4. I accompanied him on this hunt, which included an unsettling occurrence—the dying moose gave off a death rattle. George was upset by the noise and explained to me that the death rattle of a moose is a sign of impending death among the hunter's kin.[4] He did not think it signified his own death but was not entirely certain, thinking that less probable than the death of someone related to him. He quickly butchered the moose,[5] stopping at one point to say, "Maybe that's why I been so lucky, somebody's gonna die on me." We loaded my little canoe with the hide and as much meat as we could take and paddled back to camp (the motor was again defunct), not arriving until very late. George went right to his father's tent even before unloading the meat. As he told his parents of the rattle they both became visibly upset.

Paul began to question George systematically about the hunt, the killing of the moose, and the placing of the shot that killed it. He asked George to repeat parts of the story and interrupted to seek specific details that George had not volunteered. His questioning came to center on the placement of the shot. He even asked me what I had heard and seen and where I thought the shot had struck the moose. When he was certain the bullet had hit the neck in such a way as to damage the windpipe,[6] he told everyone not to worry. A bullet striking there can produce a noise like George heard simply as a result of the force with which it hits and the damage it causes. For the death rattle to have been an omen, it would have to have been attributable to something other than the mechanical effect of the bullet's impact upon the respiratory system. Everyone was relieved and George kept on with his moose hunting. Before he finally left, he killed five moose and systematically distributed their hides throughout the camp.

On July 6, a turbo-Beaver floatplane flew in and the fish camp was inspected. The camp was declared substandard and its operating license was suspended.

We expected Virginia and her husband, Eddy to join us on July 11. George wanted to use their plane for his move so he would only have to pay charges for the short flight from South Lake to Foxholm Lake and back. If he had to have a plane come from the village he would have to pay for the entire distance, a more than $500 differential that he could ill-afford. All the women but Ann were now talking about moving to Foxholm Lake. Paul said he would move up there with the same plane instead of remaining here for Virginia and Eddy's visit. He thought they might come on to Foxholm Lake with their children.

Wellington's withdrawal into his immediate family was a statement about his relations with the rest of the camp, and George was conspicuously breaking the public form of the sexual division of labor. He assisted his wife with her work on one of the moosehides and helped her cut dry meat from the last moose he had killed. In part this might be explained away by referring to his lengthy stay with Et∨en-che, who did not pay much attention to Chipewyan conventions, assuming this association made him more willing to help Joan. Men are most likely to help their wives in tasks like these when they are in isolation in the bush. George was making a statement — intentionally or not — of a commitment to his immediate family that overrode his concern for the opinion held by the rest of the camp. This period was like a replay of late May. The camp remained physically intact, but socially it was now just a series of independent families sharing a location, although a new pattern of two groups was beginning to emerge.[7]

George and his wife were packed and waiting for Virginia and Eddy's plane on July 11. They were also packed and waiting on the 12th, 13th, 14th, and 15th. George was afraid to go too far from camp lest he be unable to get back in time when the plane did come. He stopped moose hunting and turned to gathering "good rock," something that could be done near camp.

Good rock is anything the Chipewyan think is of value to a prospector although the idiom is almost always gold. Their understanding of geology varies greatly, but they are keen and careful observers of their environment with an eye for the unusual. The idea is not to start a mine although they too have fantasies of wealth. Once it is decided if a specimen is good rock or not, it is almost always thrown away. They often throw away good rock that is in fact valuable ore. Paul once sent off to be assayed what he thought was gold ore, a chunk of quartz the size of his fist taken from a wide vein running from far on shore to deep into a lake. The sample contained sufficient gold to pay the assay charges and result in a small check being mailed to him. For years afterward he received letters from the assay office asking for larger samples. He told us where the vein was located and what it looked like, proud that he had correctly identified the good rock.

Jean was anxious for the plane to come so she could take it back to the village when it finished its ferry trips to Foxholm Lake. She was now ill, but Miley was so lazy she still had to do all of the work, including hauling water from the lake and gathering the firewood for cooking. It was too warm to keep fires going in the tent stoves but fires were sometimes needed outside to cook and to heat water to wash clothes. The demand for firewood was minimal, but all the readily accessible firewood had long since been gathered.

By July 18, the lack of a plane was a general annoyance. We had eaten up all of the small game in the vicinity and there was no fresh meat in camp. Store supplies were running low again with George out of almost everything. The fish nets, which never got more than desultory attention anyway, were yielding just about enough to feed the dogs every couple of days. In theory an ideal summer feed is about two pounds of fish every other day, but the dogs' diet now was far more erratic. They seemed to get by on about a third of the ideal diet but they were steadily losing weight. If a day's yield was exceptionally high they might get an eight to ten pound fish only then to have to fast for a week.

The fish nets provided an interesting example of the limits of the conflict and the overriding importance of kinship even during a time of redefinition of relationships. There were three nets in camp, one of Wellington's, one of George's, and one of Paul's. If Miley had a net it was not in the water.[8] Wellington's net was the only one to have been set and was checked sporadically. A daily check was desirable but every two days was more realistic. He picked from the fish he brought back those that would go to feed his dogs, still tethered down by the shore where he kept the boat. He would tell his father, or more frequently the children would tell his father and everyone else in camp, what kind of fish and how many of each the net yielded. Eventually Paul would go and take for his dogs what he needed from the fish left after Wellington had fed his own animals. The rest of the fish were left on the shore where George would go and get what he needed for his three dogs. Wellington and George never said a word to each other about the fish and never came into contact near them.[9]

The women occasionally went berry picking and made a few other trips for special things, more for entertainment than anything else. On a fruitless trip to look for sea gull eggs, something May particularly liked, they captured some baby terns. Every tent had to have a baby tern, replacing the baby mergansers that had not survived our ministrations earlier in the season. As had been the case with the ducks, catching minnows to feed them became a source of entertainment for the children and the younger women.

When no airplane came on July 19, Paul, at George's insistence, began making divinations with caribou scapula, seeking partly to determine the arrival date of a plane but mostly to help hold George in camp. This lasted several days and eventually involved some of the women. There were no useful predictive results although George did stay while the process continued. This form of divination is a technique rather than *inkoze* and therefore open to anyone independent of gender. I have seen children make divinations this way but not without an adult watching.

The sameness was broken one day when Paul saw something coming up from the south on the lake. Eventually we realized it was a party of canoeists, and we paddled out to meet them. They were a group of school teachers from St. Paul, Minnesota on a wilderness trip along the river system that flows northeastward through South Lake. They were holding to a day by day schedule, one planned out in advance down to the hour they would rise and when they would stop for each meal. They were proud that they had yet to portage a rapids on the first 130 or so miles of their trip. They refused our invitation to join us for lunch. We later found where they had stopped to eat a mile or so past our camp. They kept complaining, as we paddled alongside them, that they had lost too much time one morning, oversleeping after celebrating a birthday.

Since their vision of this place was different from ours and did not include us or any kind of visiting, we warned them to be careful of the rapids at the north end of the lake and returned home. George was a little miffed that he had not had the nerve to try to mooch some cigarettes from them. It is always difficult to get precise details on the stories that travel through the north, but later in the fall we made inquiries about just who these people were. Their pride in making it through rapids without portaging came a cropper later in their trip and one of them drowned. The tragedy of the death was intensified when a passing black bear lunched on the victim while the others were downstream attempting to recover their gear. I do wish I could say that those of us who went out in the boats to greet them were properly stunned by the tragedy, but we did try to keep a somber mien as the details were recounted to us.

Paul finally finished rebuilding the old freight canoe, and George was again talking of moving to Foxholm Lake. He planned to depart on July 21, and it took a good deal of persuasion to get him to wait a bit longer for the airplane. Paul knew full well an airplane coming up heavily laden with Virginia and her family could not carry the extra gasoline it would need to make all these ferry trips. The thought should have crossed my mind but didn't. I don't know about George, but he should have known. His supplies were getting short and he was anxious to go. He was familiar with the area only from his winter travels, so he used this time to work out a route from the only map we had. He chose the shortest route in spite of several long portages along it. Rain on the twenty-first kept him from making an impulsive move. It seemed to be a good day to avoid boats, as later that day while we were chasing ducklings on a small lake, he leaned too far overboard trying to reach one and managed to upset the canoe. In his ambivalence he decided to cancel the trip on the twenty-second, citing the heavy infestation of black flies, the heat, the hardship of the trip for the children, and his fear for the safety of his family. He tried to get me to make the trip with him and I rather liked the idea, but my wife was wisely having none of it.

Wellington kept silent on the whole business in spite of the fact that he had extensive knowledge of the area and had traveled through much of it in both summer and winter. He knew the landmarks to use at each season and what routes to take to avoid the longest portages. If he made any comments about his brother's planned route, they did not get to me and I saw no sign of them in Paul's words or deeds. Paul began a new series of divinations to predict the date of arrival of the airplane, making two on the twenty-second. On the morning of the twenty-third, George announced that the mosquitoes were too bad to go that day. At noon a thunderstorm hit leaving high waves on the lake. That seemed to make travel impossibly dangerous and to settle the issue for the day, but either something happened or George had just reached the limits of his patience. He had put his fish net in the lake shortly after his father had finished the canoe and at 3:00 P.M. he went and brought it in. By 4:05 he was packed and ready to depart for Foxholm Lake. Into that small sixteen foot freight canoe he put: Joan, two children, little Ann to care for the baby, three sled dogs, the tent, bedding, the stove and stovepipe, food, a fish net, several suitcases, rifles, the baby tern in a cage made of mosquito netting and sticks, and numerous other supplies including axes, knives, dog chains, fishing rods, plates and cutlery, utensils, and lamps. Loading the canoe involved a lot of packing and unpacking, kibitzing about weight and balance, choice of routes, and just plain general advice.

The reactions to his sudden decision to depart again reveal some of the contrasts between individuals in the camp. May was worried about the safety of her son and his family. Her own life had involved many seasons of canoe travel and the traumatic deaths of several close relatives in canoe accidents. These were not half-remembered stories, as they were to her children, but intense memories of pain and hurt. She had a realistic understanding of the very real hazards of a trip like this. Less than two months ago these lakes had been filled with ice water and in a few more months they would again be ice water. What would be a minor accident in southerly climes is fatal in these lakes. If the boat capsizes more than a short distance from land, you don't swim to shore, you die. Quickly.

Paul also knew and felt the pain of past deaths, but he was male and his concerns were different from May's. Gender roles do sometimes make very different demands on people. He was quietly confident his son could make the trip and offered George advice about his novice cross-country move by canoe as a father and head of a family. Paul had been making moves like this all his life. He knew that while it did not do to underplay the danger, it was even more likely to be fatal for a man not to know what he was capable of doing. A realistic judgment of one's own capabilities and the demands made by a situation cannot come from words alone. For the sake of himself and of his family, George had much to learn about himself that could come only from doing.

Miley wandered about during the loading, but Wellington refused to participate, remaining in his tent as did Jean. They were kept informed by glances out the front of their tents, overheard conversations, and the constant movement of children throughout the camp.

Dogs play an important symbolic role in the culture, Savishinsky's (1975) work has shown that dogs are a reflection of the pride men feel in themselves and of their perception of their social image. When it came time to load George's dogs into the canoe, the role of these animals in individual self-imagery was obvious. Wellington was proud of his dogs, a pride based on a team of young, fast, strong dogs of matched color. He did not seek the wildness or the impetuousness that feature in stories the unmarried men tell of their dog teams, but the same strength and endurance in a more disciplined form. He did not encourage viciousness in his dogs and there were many nice animals among them, but neither was he gentle with them. He regarded sled dogs not as pets but things to be used, traded, or discarded like any other valuable tool.[10]

George's attachment to his dogs was different and deeper, exposing a sentimentality apparently lacking in his brother. He was extremely proud of the team which now consisted of three surviving members of a litter obtained from EtΘen-che, dogs far larger than the local ones, as EtΘen-che bred for size. George encouraged them to be vicious, and one of his team was a notorious killer of other dogs. He was far harsher in his treatment of his dogs than was Wellington. Pride, attachment, and caring are not always expressed in affection. His pride came from their size, strength, viciousness, and their being littermates. He felt this gave them a moral superiority over teams of mixed ancestry and created in him expectations of superior behavior. I do not fully understand his particular understanding of the deep metaphors that were involved here. His dogs were more than five years old, long past the optimum age for Chipewyan sled dogs. Their teeth were badly worn and they showed other signs of their age. Three dogs is three less than the ideal for a dog team. That he continued to use them was evidence of that sentimentality he allowed to interfere with his performance.

As with *inkoze*, valuable possessions, and (I think I understand Chipewyan men correctly) women, what is most desired is not always the easiest to keep or to control (Slobodin 1960, 1975). At least three times George's dogs had attacked and tried to kill him. When it came time to load the first dog into the canoe, he could not get it to obey, even with a savage beating. George was forced to turn to Paul—Paul, who kept only old dogs and discards other people gave him, in order to find three animals tractable enough to be carried in the canoe.

George's departure left behind a palpable wall of fear and tension enclosing the camp. His canoe was so heavily laden with his dependents and possessions that it had minimal freeboard. The lake still had four-to-six-inch waves as an aftershock of the thunderstorm and a few large waves crested at over a foot. Taken wrongly, any of the larger waves could flood over the side of the canoe and consign its occupants to memory. The two paddles were cumbersome homemade ones of narrow birch, not six inches at their widest point. Joan, seated at the front, had a child to cope with and little practice or endurance with a canoe paddle. George, standing or sitting in the rear, had little control over the cumbersome boat. May watched her son's departure until he circled a hook point a quarter-mile away, passing there from our view.

The chance of an accident on this journey was great, but it was not concern for George's fate that sent all but May scurrying to their tents. She was wrought with fear as she returned to her own tent, and fear is but a shade removed from anger. Paul, probably through some otherwise innocuous remark expressing confidence in George, provided the spark that set her off. He became the target for all her emotion: it was his fault George was leaving and had committed his and other lives to such a foolish venture. The slights and wrongs of thirty-five years of marriage were expressed in shouts and accusations booming over the huddled offspring skulking in the dubious privacy of their tents. Paul responded quickly, but the depth of his emotion had not been tried as had May's and he soon lapsed into silence.

When May could sustain expression of the vehemence of her feelings no longer, she took Barb and walked a few hundred feet to the edge of the woods at the back of camp. She remained there until after 7:00 P.M. before returning. The cloud of her anger lasted the night and into the morrow.

The relationship between women and public power is rarely as one-sided as it now seems fashionable to assert. May was bound by gender role and unable to prevent George's departure upon what, however dangerous, was a normal male prerogative, but the bonds of sentiment, carefully played, are powerful. Her explosive anger at Paul cowed the entire camp, but the outburst was also an effective manipulation of the structure of her family. She was threatened by the conflict between her sons now escalating into a permanent breach of relations between them, one that would sunder the family she and Paul had created.

The marriage between Paul and May was the pivot by which her children had related themselves to each other throughout their lives. By making her outburst an attack upon Paul, she raised the spectre of that pivot breaking. Threatening to intensify the threat of schism to the point where the structural link that connected all of these people collapsed into chaos, she forced George and Wellington to be seen by everyone there not as autonomous adult males who were brothers, but as her children who belonged within her family. From the moment of her explosion the pressure was upon Wellington to heal, however unwillingly, the breach with George. They were equally her sons and any relationship between them would have to accommodate their shared relationship to her. Their mother would tolerate nothing else.

1. Joan had ruined the only moosehide they had by leaving it to soak in the lake too long, which caused it to rot. Tanning a moosehide is a difficult, complex, and time consuming task that most women under thirty have refused to learn. As was seen in Ann's dry meat making, women's work and skills are a bottleneck in the production process that regulate, directly and indirectly, the extractive efforts of the men.

2. That a moosehide finally triggered the conflict into the open is not as surprising as it may seem. Moosehide is always in demand. Besides the embroidered or beaded finery made from it, it has no substitute in the manufacture of durable mitts, gloves, or moccasins for use in the cold of winter. Tanned hide is always scarce. Never enough moose are killed to meet the demands of the village, even without taking into consideration the animal's age, sex, and time of the year it is killed, all of which affect the desirability of individual hides. Killing a moose on South Lake was unusual. Paul insisted he had not seen moose or their sign here more than three times in his life. This was probably an overstatement but his experience led him to believe moose were uncommon here and that there was little prospect of obtaining another hide before winter. As it turned out, moose were common that year, but no one knew it at the time.

3. Wellington did not want the snowmobile. A more dispassionate judge of machinery than George, he realized the model I had was too large and heavy to suit his own pattern of snowmobile use.

4. Chipewyan thought about omens does not tend toward the pleasant. Actions that involve manipulation of *inkoze* threaten the performer, as *inkoze* not handled flawlessly has the nasty habit of rebounding upon the performer, whereas other brushes with the supernatural, like George's moose, tend to have their consequences on the kin of the person in contact. This work is not the place to venture deeper into the nature of *inkoze*, but such situations rather obviously generate a level of concern about a man's actions and their consequences that combine with a feeling of helplessness. Who can ever know when these things might happen?

5. Relatively speaking. Moose often weigh over half-a-ton and it takes several hours to butcher one correctly.

6. The cervical vertebrae inward from the point of impact were smashed—the lethal part of the damage.

7. The emerging pattern, which was never actualized, was (1) Wellington and Ann with their children plus Jean and her sons. (2) Paul and May and their dependents plus George and Joan and their children. My economic functioning was as an extension of Paul's household. This allowed George a greater freedom of action, as he could differentially ally with either Paul or me. In the fall we were joined by Paul's father-in-law, putting George into a loose alliance with his household while I retained mine with Paul's.

8. Miley had lost his rifle in a card game before he came north and had not been able to replace it. He was woefully unprepared for the bush.

9. Paul would mediate between his sons, making sure that over a few days Wellington always left enough fish. He never took so many for his own dogs that George's went hungry for too long.

10. It may be worth noting that the Indians are full of stories of whites who treated their dogs like pets and ended up with unreliable, slow, and intractable teams whose ineptness posed a hazard to their owners. I choose not to defend Chipewyan methods of dog care, but because systems are structured by symbols and metaphor does not mean they are not well-honed to meet functional requirements.

# Chapter Eight

Virginia and Eddy arrived the day after George left, but our planned move north had to be abandoned immediately. The aircraft that brought them was a Cessna 185, too small to do the ferry work and without adequate gasoline to even try. All of us had to remain at South Lake until their holiday was finished. Arrangements were quickly made for Virginia and Eddy's pick-up to be made by a deHaviland Beaver that would bring drums of spare gasoline for us to move the day they returned to the village. While Jean and Miley loaded their belongings into the 185 we persuaded the pilot to swing north after take off to look for George; a courtesy for which he later billed us $50.

The makeup of our camp had changed in the last two days. George, Joan, their two small children, and little Ann had left for Foxholm Lake. Jean and Miley had gone back to the village. Camp now consisted of Wellington and Ann with their three children, Paul and May with Phil and Mike, and Eddy and Virginia with their two small children and the baby. Barb divided her time between her mother's and grandmother's tents. There were nineteen people in camp, including my family and eleven of them were children. Before these changes the entire camp had consisted of interrelated people. Seven people had left, five arrived, and the camp still consisted entirely of interrelated people.

Virginia had lost her treaty status[1] with her first marriage, but Eddy had been nontreaty since birth. His father was a clerk in the Hudson's Bay Company store at the administrative center near the village and had always said that he had had to surrender his treaty status before the company would hire him. Eddy and his brothers had grown up in a life style directed toward jobs rather than bush living. He saw the bush as a place to gather food and relax, a change of pace from his daily life rather than as the source of his livelihood. The mechanics of forming functional alliances of bush households were not a factor in his perception of social life. Neither he nor Virginia had any sympathy for those concerns, but they did share the kinship system and its ideas about relationships. It was to these, almost idealized since they were never tested by sustained bush life, that they turned to base their actions and words.

The split between Wellington and George was an accomplished fact, shifting concern to ensuring the solidarity of the now nonresidential kin ties. Eddy and Virginia added to the pressure that was being placed upon Wellington to heal the rift. They had not been here during the spring and early summer while the conflict was developing, hence its tension and emotion had no meaning to them. They were concerned solely with preserving the ties of kinship and sentiment between kin to whom they were equally related. This is a classic problem of kinship: ties of kinship are often not compartmentalized in such a way as to provide a basis for taking sides in a dispute. The issue between the conflicting parties becomes secondary to the nature of the relationship to the parties involved in the dispute. If the relationship to both sides is the same, then the decision whether to preserve or to terminate those relationship(s) is the paramount issue.

After being separated for several months, the people began trying to catch up on the events in each others lives. This was not a hunting unit but merely a temporary summer aggregation fated to disperse in three weeks within which the past contest for autonomy and control now made no sense. In these conversations Eddy and Virginia reinterpreted the events of the past few weeks to reflect their own social positions and values. A general consensus emerged that conflict between Wellington and George was foolish.

To Wellington, the only one present to whom judgment and call to reconciliation could be given, fell the burden of repairing the breach between him and his poor brother; a brother off alone in the bush without supplies or human contact and perhaps already the victim of some terrible accident.

While the camp was renegotiating the events of the spring, verbally constructing a new reality, and directing their will upon Wellington to see it implemented, the stories of *bekaycho* were told and retold. *Bekaycho* was old hat to those who had been with us in the spring, but to the newcomers it was new ground with a fascination of its own. Eddy reacted, as he almost always reacted to new things, with glee. It was possible to pull him aside and get him quietly to talk of *bekaycho* and he would do so seriously and with quiet passion. Then would come that grin as he watched for the effect of his words.

If *bekaycho* was another story for Eddy's entertainment, Virginia displayed an absolute fascination with it. She had spent more time outside than the others, was more proficient in English, and was better able to relate what she heard to the English–Canadian cultural context. Virginia sought specific information about Bigfoot itself from my wife and children. Her search for information brought forth a hoard of hitherto hidden information that included the sightings in Vancouver. This information carried its own validity, and I am not sure that it was effectively conveyed to Virginia that the sightings were known hoaxes. Her interest in Bigfoot helped drag *bekaycho* back into public attention. Barb, who had been in camp since June, shared her mother's interest. She and little Ann were at an age at which they knew most of the fears, concerns, and worries of adults and may have been better informed about the doings of other people than any one else in camp. They knew they would soon have to face many of these issues in their own lives but they still had only the judgment of children to guide them. Their lack of experience sometimes led them to curious conclusions about the meaning of those matters of concern to the adults.

July 24 brought an unwelcome surprise in the form of an RCMP visit. The Chipewyan do not welcome intrusion by the RCMP or others of official Canada into the bush beyond the margins of the village. We are now conditioned to accept that the symbols, ideas, and language of alien cultures are ways of knowing the environment within which they dwell, but we have conveniently managed to subordinate the significance of that understanding to our quest for objectivity. These things are not passive ways of perceiving a determined positivist reality but a mode of interaction shared between the *dene* and their environment. All animate life interacts and, to a greater or lesser degree, affects the life and behavior of all other animate forms. In their deliberate and splendid isolation, the Chipewyan interact with all life in accordance with their understanding, and the animate universe responds. White Canada does not come silently and openly into the bush in search of understanding or communion, it sojourns briefly in the full glory of its colonial power to exploit and regulate all animate being and foremost of all, the *dene*. It comes asserting a clashing alien causality certain in the fundamentalist exercise of the power of its belief. It talks too loudly, its posture is wrong, its movement harsh and graceless; it does not know what to see and it hears nothing. Its presence brings a stunning confusion heard deafeningly in a growing circle of silence created by a confused and disordered animate universe.[2]

Miley had returned to the village telling stories of the argument between Paul and May. These stories had percolated to the RCMP detachment and had become transformed into a violent fight between Paul and George. The vaunted RCMP thoroughness is not solely a feature of legend. They had come sniffing in pursuit of this man— shades of the legends of the mad trapper— who had had to flee into the bush to escape the consequences of the violence done to his father. They were satisfied once the situation had been explained to them, and when asked if they could locate George, they informed us they were unable to do so. They had insufficient gasoline to make a search and besides, the cost of the charter had been billed to the Mission band. The RCMP only come when they can justify the time and expenditure to the accountants who audit their books and they said they could not justify a further expenditure of funds in the absence of a crime. They did agree to carry a message back to Fred requesting that he send more supplies and a plane to locate George. The RCMP then departed and, always prepared for the exigencies of bush life, landed just south of the big island and spent the afternoon fishing.

Wellington yielded to his mother's fears and agreed to take my canoe (and me) and go look for George. Our search took three days and we found George's trail where he had reached the long portage on his second day of travel. Wellington there recovered one of his traps abandoned several years before. He did not think highly of George's route, pointing out that the long portage had to be made through thick spruce scrub. Backtracking over part of his route to the camp George had made on his first night, Wellington then took a shorter route back to South Lake. He seemed to harbor no fear for

his brother's safety. He had decided to abandon South Lake himself
before the fall hunting season and was using this trip to search for a
place to build a new cabin. Our search route made a loop through a
series of lakes he thought likely cabin sites. He chose to build the
new cabin where we first found sign of George's passing.

By the end of July, people back in the village were anticipating the
arrival of caribou in the far north. The increasing income level in the
village gave some people the funds for hunting trips in charter aircraft. It made sense for these people to stop by our camp and obtain
firsthand word of the caribou and whatever dry meat we would give
them. The caribou did not come down to South Lake until October,
but we had a steady stream of visitors until we moved north. At
Foxholm Lake they continued to come until the lakes began to freeze.
Our concern for George diminished, as their comings and goings
brought a plethora of aircraft and the knowledge that emergency transportation was available. One plane stopped by on its way to
EtΘen-che's camp, and Wellington took a day trip up and back. He
returned with word that caribou had arrived at treeline and that a
large party of archaeologists had stopped at EtΘen-che's. In due time
Fred sent a plane to bring us supplies. He had made arrangements for
the band to pay part of the cost. The passengers on this flight, including a new RCMP constable, were along as compensation to the band
for its financial involvement. None of these people were familiar with
the South Lake–Foxholm Lake area although all of them knew of
EtΘen-che and had heard about his camp. They took Wellington along
with them to give them the benefit of his firsthand knowledge of the
area and his knowledge of George's probable routes.

Wellington had already made the day trip to EtΘen-che's camp and
knew that archaeologists were in the area. He had not met them before
they scattered to their survey areas, but his aunt had indicated they
were "nice people." He was not quite sure what an archaeologist did,
but the relevant fact was that transient whites were in the area and
traveling by canoe. There was no discernible interest in the archaeologists at this time, no attribution of any of the typical bogeyman
characteristics to them, and no concern about where they might have
gone after they left EtΘen-che's.

## EtΘen-che

Caribou-tail, so known to the Chipewyan for the hood of an old coat he wore years ago, is the stuff of legend. Born in Montana around the turn of the century, he dropped out of school in his teens when he learned that he could earn more in a single day trapping coyotes for fur and bounty than an adult could earn in a week. Drafted into the army, he spent World War I at Schofield Barracks in Hawaii. After the war he returned to Montana and served an apprenticeship during the 1920s in the extensive and highly publicized campaigns to trap the last American wolves from the Dakota badlands. Here he learned the use of poison. Killing wolves became an end unto itself, a crusade whose goal was the elimination of the last wild member of the species. He had great practical knowledge of how to find and kill wolves, but very little understanding of the beasts themselves or their part in an ecological system. His one great fear was that they would "get him;" that when the time came for him to die, there would still live free wolves.

He moved north to Alberta after the wolves were gone from the Lower 48 and for years ran a trapline out of Edmonton. As that area began to urbanize, he moved farther and farther north. He worked the boreal forest near Mission before finally moving his base camp to the very edge of the trees in the Northwest Territories. He married during this part of his life but his wife had a touch of the fancy women in her; unsuited to wilderness life she soon departed. He had been living with May's sister for years when I first met him at Christmas, 1969.

His well-funded operation was a constant source of irritation to George who was never able to reconcile himself to EtΘen-che having so much while he was always running short himself. EtΘen-che's most productive years in recent times were those when George and Fred were with him to do the work. Some years EtΘen-che poisoned more than four-hundred wolves, recovering less than half of them. His legal yearly income in the early 1970s was in excess of $15,000, nearly five times the combined total income of all Mission Chipewyan who trapped in the Northwest Territories. EtΘen-che also had a substantial hidden income from the illegal sale of tanned, white wolf hide trophies to tourists and local businessmen. Using a network of carefully maintained contacts, he hosted hunting expeditions for wealthy outsiders, unbothered by the area's formal status as a game sanctuary.

EtΘen-che could be an engaging and charming host. He was generous with his supplies and equipment and was a mandatory stop for any government or scientific party in the region. For years the games played by EtΘen-che and May's sister as each hid their whiskey bottles from the other were a delight to their knowing visitors. EtΘen-che was also a stingy and suspicious man with a disdain for the truth that would make a riverboat gambler blanch. George saw this side of him more than any other.

As EtΘen-che neared the end of his days, his suspicion and dislike of the outside became a desperate determination to die and be buried at his camp on the tundra's edge. He lost this battle, expiring in a hospital and lying buried in civilization after the plane carrying his remains north was forced back by bad weather. There were no funds for a second try. He lost also his great battle with the wolf. They survive him still upon the tundra but their future seems no more comforting than was his end.

The aircraft flew to the cabins at Foxholm Lake, but no one was there. Wellington knew George intended to get supplies from EtΘen-che so he directed the aircraft to fly over the usual canoe routes between the two camps. They found them crossing the last small lake before Bear Lake, the large lake on the south side of the esker where EtΘen-che had his camp. George had his entire family with him. He was still hurting from the accident that had happened during his move and was desperately glad for resupply and contact. While the supplies were being unloaded and the people socialized, George began to tell the Chipewyan of his encounters with *bekaycho* at Foxholm Lake. In meetings between mixed parties of Chipewyan and whites the two ethnic groups usually talk separately in their own language without simultaneous translation. The whites would not know what George was saying unless someone later chose to tell them. *Bekaycho* was known only to our camp and whomever Jean, Miley, and Mickey might have told about it back at Mission. Considering the accuracy of the stories that were told back there about George's departure, I doubt that any of the stories about *bekaycho* had spread very far. The other Chipewyan on the plane did not have any idea what George was talking about. I don't think George and Wellington were really on speaking terms, saying only the minimum that form required.

Wellington reached our camp fairly bursting with laughter. I don't know what he told the rest of the people on the plane about *bekaycho*, but he did not tell them anything about it until after they had left George. Neither was he able to make George understand the significance of the archaeologists. He related his younger brother's stories of *bekaycho* with delight, laughing at George's discomfort over such a foolish thing as passing archaeologists. Even the women and children, that part of this population most likely to accept the reality of creatures lurking in the bush, did not connect the archaeologists with what George had seen. The archaeologists had visited with a kinswoman and had enjoyed her hospitality; their social identity was known even though no one here had actually met them. I am inclined to think that Wellington alone put the pieces together, recognizing that George must have encountered them and thought that they were *bekaycho*. He did not say that to me until several days later and I am sure that it was an expression of his sense of humor to let everyone else run on in speculation about what it was that George had encountered.

*Bekaycho*'s reemergence began another round of stories. The now old stories of the spring had added to them stories of how May's sister had seen, and sometimes shot at, strange white men lurking near their camp. These stories were not equated with *bekaycho*, although the suggestion was made. May's sister's drinking habits gave her little credibility and the adults thought it more likely that what she had seen were bear. Virginia's reaction was much like her earlier one, fascination coupled with a questioning attitude toward the specific events. She was concerned by the stories and whatever it was her brother was seeing. Her attitude did not carry over to Eddy.

The behavior of the men of this camp toward *bekaycho* was marked by their not worrying about the reality of *bekaycho* lurking out there beyond the camp while understanding the form and being able to manipulate it. Eddy played all the stories by the context of the situation in which he found himself at the moment. When he was with people who worried about it, he treated the stories seriously; when he dealt with the camp's children he went so far as to embellish the events and ferocity of *bekaycho*. When speaking with Paul he was more circumspect but remained unworried about what had happened to George. Dealing with Wellington and me, he was delighted with the stories; treating them as valued jokes and trying to elicit laughter with them. He was capable of, and willing to, give *bekaycho* whatever credibility the situation called for and he would act upon or toward *bekaycho* in the same manner.

From Eddy's standpoint the significant information was the presence of caribou at Foxholm Lake. He had come north for caribou on his holidays and they were already half over; if the caribou weren't going to come here to him, he was going to go there to them. Wellington and Eddy began to plan a quick trip to Foxholm Lake in my canoe. Wellington drolly explained that he and Eddy were going to see what "was bothering George." They hoped to reach the cabins within two days. The supply plane had found George on the evening of July 29, and within forty-eight hours Eddy and Wellington were well en route. They left South Lake in fine spirit and with high expectations. They were going caribou hunting in a place where caribou were known to be. For two men traveling with a minimum of equipment through this marvelously untouched country, the trip had all the joy of a pilgrimage. Just to shed the bonds of camp or village and vanish into the bush brings a joy that runs deep into the soul of even the most insensitive Chipewyan men. Many Chipewyan women share this joy of escape into a realm beyond the confines of the mundane and it is a bane of their lives that they so rarely have the freedom to exercise it. The two men made rapid progress. Gambling on the water level in a stream, they took a different route than George had. The stream's water level proved to be lower than they had hoped and rocks exposed in its bed bode ill for their return laden with meat, but they were young and strong and the prospect of a little extra portaging discouraged them not at all. They made Foxholm Lake the second day although later than they had expected.

It was so late when George departed South Lake on July 23, that he only had time to paddle to the north end of the lake and make the first short portage before stopping to set camp. The waves remained high for a few hours after he left, forcing him to travel along the shore and follow around the bays rather than cutting across their mouths. He had only marginal control of the canoe, having to stand up in the back in order to make any kind of headway at all. He later said that Joan's effort with the paddle greatly increased their speed but that she tired easily and continually had to divert her attention to the children. The next day he made a series of short portages through a chain of small lakes under conditions that were far from ideal. The weather remained hot and the insects were at their summer peak, a constant torment for the children who were both sick again.[3]

George's hope of having the dogs pack the goods over the portages evolved out of his earlier plan to have them pull the toboggan across, but both ideas proved to be more trouble than they were worth. At the end of the second day he put his net in the water to catch some fish. The third day involved two short portages that were followed by the long one where Wellington and I had found his trail. George was making such poor time on his trip that Wellington mistook his third day's travel for the second day's. The long portage on the third day proved that George's choice of route had been in error. He had deliberately chosen to make this single, long portage instead of going by a route with more but shorter portages. The long portage was a good several miles before it reached the lake–river chain that ended by the cabins at Foxholm Lake. It began in open ground that led into a scrub spruce forest before reaching parkland timber on high ground then winding down through thick brush to the shore.

When the Chipewyan have to portage a canoe they lace the paddles into a "V" inside the boat. The shafts of the paddles sit one on each shoulder to bear the weight of the canoe. This arrangement is not very stable and depends upon the tightness of the lashings to hold the paddles in place. Sweat and fatigue, especially in hot weather, can produce carelessness in securing the paddles. If the canoe slips or falls the paddles can produce a scissorlike motion against the neck of the person carrying the canoe. The cumbersomeness of this arrangement is enhanced by the practice of carrying the rifle inside the inverted canoe in case they run into bear or something worse while their vision is cut off.

In the course of the long portage, which George had to make many times to get all the freight across, the canoe slipped. It had absorbed water since Paul had finished it and was now quite heavy. The blow struck him near the collar bone. The bone itself did not break but there was severe bruising and some internal injury. He was in immediate pain and said later that he was spitting up pus until well into September. In spite of the injury he felt that he had no choice but to continue the trip, doing all of the packing while Joan and little Ann coped with the children. By the time he got everything down to the shore, he was so tired that they set the tent and rested there for a day. They had plenty of dried meat, took small game along the way, and had the fish net to get fish to feed the dogs, but they were out of flour, lard, tea, sugar, and tobacco. The rest of the trip took two days but did not require any more portages. There were several rapids to cross, but a rope could be used to pull the the canoe through them so that it did not have to be unpacked each time. As they neared the cabins they saw caribou and George killed a bull. Being among the caribou relieved their immediate concerns, but they were so tired that they did not bother to clean up the cabin, resting instead in the tent for several days.

As soon as George felt stronger he took the freight canoe over to the main lake and began to hunt caribou. On this hunt he first saw *bekaycho*'s footprints on a sand and gravel point where the west bay of Foxholm Lake narrows into a small channel that opens eastward into the main part of the lake. He was puzzled by the footprints and curious about a hole dug into the ground at the top edge of the collapsing west face of the esker. He was not particularly worried by these signs, as he was armed and hunting, but later told me he had had some concern about leaving his family alone back at the cabins. Various scientific and government parties make occasional excursions into these lakes in spite of their remoteness. The cost of charter aircraft is so high that it is often too expensive for such groups to fly out otherwise serviceable supplies and equipment when they leave. Over the years they have left behind their sign in accumulated trash. The presence of yet another unknown outsider on this lake was not troublesome in and of itself.

George killed several bull caribou and packed the meat down to the sand point on the narrows where he piled and covered it. He was still too weak to load it into the canoe, paddle back to the beach at the south end of the bay, and then pack it the nearly half-mile to the cabins that same day. He took only the most perishable cuts of meat with him after making sure that the rest was well covered. Sea gulls were abundant now and many ravens had already come south with the caribou herd, so he had to take special care to keep them off the meat. These large birds quickly ruin any exposed meat by pecking deep holes into it and eliminating waste as they walk and squabble over it.

He returned to the meat pile the following day and found that it had been scattered around the point. The birds had gotten to the now exposed meat and had fouled it beyond use. There were fresh *bekaycho* tracks all over the point. Since there seemed to be plenty of caribou, he could afford the loss of the meat, but a cache had been ruined to no apparent purpose since no meat seemed to be missing. Disgusted, he returned to camp feeling ill-will toward a creature that would destroy a cache and let birds foul the meat. This was a violation of Chipewyan ideas about a cache, which we saw earlier, affected Joan's position in camp, and borders on animal abuse of the kind caribou find offensive. They could have become sufficiently enraged to have deserted the Foxholm Lake area for years.

The following day, July 29, George felt well enough to make the trip to EtΘen-che's for an interim supply of store foodstuffs and staples. This was going to be an expensive proposition, as EtΘen-che charged dearly for what he did not give away, but it would tide them over until they could be resupplied. EtΘen-che had a working high-frequency radio George could use to order supplies and a plane to bring them. The trip to EtΘen-che's was nearly as long as the one from South Lake to Foxholm Lake, but it was not nearly as difficult a trip to make. George and his family were to go from the cabins to Foxholm Lake, then overland for several miles through a series of small lakes, and then on to and west along Bear Lake. They could leave the canoe on Bear Lake and walk the last few miles over firm ground. He had years of experience in this area and knew the route well in all seasons, so it seemed like a simple journey. Foxholm Lake is so close to treeline that the insects were gone, removing that annoyance.[4]

They had made the worst part of the journey and were starting the last portage to Bear Lake when the supply aircraft found them. He and his family were relieved by the resupply, but George found the experience somewhat frustrating. He tried to tell the passengers on the plane of *bekaycho* but no one reacted to his stories; his account of the disturbed meat pile was heard but its meaning was not understood. Perturbed by their lack of understanding, he and his family started the return trip to Foxholm Lake. By the time the plane left, it was getting late, but George elected to continue back by canoe, making the portages all over again only this time with supplies to be unloaded, packed, then reloaded at each portage.

The return trip was time consuming and George was again becoming tired. The children, too, were tired and Joan and little Ann were reaching the limits of both their patience and their endurance. Night still comes late this time of year but there are a few hours of solid darkness. There is no snow or ice to reflect the ambient light, making these nights among the darkest of the entire year. By the time they had made half the trip back to Foxholm Lake, the strain was telling on everyone. Every time he packed the canoe, carrying his rifle inside it, George thought he could see something large skulking around in the dark just at the edge of his vision. The sick and exhausted baby was crying once again when from out of the dark came a cry mocking it. The rifle in the canoe, explained by "you never know what you'll run into in this country," suddenly seemed to be an expression of wisdom proved by what could only be the mocking cry of *bekaycho*.

The canoe was dumped, the rifle was up and ready as an exhausted and exasperated George stood ready to shoot. Taking some of the supplies and abandoning the canoe, he led his wife and family off into the night. They had to detour miles out of their way to get around the lakes between them and the cabins; George always ready to shoot at the first glimpse of *bekaycho*. Tired and laden with their burdens as they were it took them hours to reach the cabins.

As they approached the cabins, they heard something rattling around in one of the buildings. George remembered when once before he had heard sounds coming from an unoccupied cabin. Memory of the Old Black Woman's death was too fresh for him to have forgotten his vow to never again fail to recognize a similar situation. The terms in which Chipewyan men think in a situation like this and the terms in which Chipewyan women think in the same situation are often very different. I do not know if he had told Joan about the incident at the bush village on Missionary Lake, but little Ann had not heard about it. George made them sit down and wait while he moved cautiously down to investigate what proved to be only a loose dog that had gotten into the cabin. Joan and little Ann were not thrilled at what they felt was George's foolishness in making them wait.

George returned for the canoe the following day and recovered it and the rest of the supplies, but otherwise he avoided Foxholm Lake, staying south of it and close to his cabin. Wellington and Eddy arrived after he had recovered the canoe and while he was avoiding the lake and any possible contact with *bekaycho*. He told them what had happened and they in turn told him of the archaeologists. Apparently neither had much effect upon the other. I think George began to fear that he might look foolish and so kept his distance from them. He did not hunt with them that first day, but did go over to Foxholm Lake with them to point out where his meat pile had been and to show them *bekaycho*'s footprints and the strange hole dug close by. He then went off by himself while Wellington and Eddy continued on for a successful hunt. They too made a meat pile on the point before returning to the cabins that night.

Wellington and Eddy went hunting again, but they did not hunt with George. Both George and Wellington had already accepted that they would continue to be brothers and that this meant cooperation, but they were not yet prepared to be graceful about it. At an affectual level the rift between them had not healed. Wellington is a harder man than George and had little reason to cease nursing his slights. Even if the state of relations between them were better than I am allowing, there was little practical logic in their hunting together. For all three of them to have taken my small canoe would have meant leaving behind even more meat for yet another trip, and my small motor was almost useless for propelling the larger freight canoe.

Eddy and Wellington needed to take meat that was to be carried, portaged, and then flown nearly 150 miles, while George was only worried about his own consumption and making dry meat. They were after specific cuts of meat, ones that could be carried, would stay fresh, and provide the highest possible ratio of fat and meat to bone. If George went over to Foxholm Lake at all after the first day, I suspect both boats were used and that Eddy and Wellington went off one way while George went off somewhere else.[5]

The second day's hunt was also successful. Some of the meat was brought back to the cabins but most of it was left on Foxholm Lake in meat piles. As the number of caribou Eddy and Wellington had killed increased, they were able to be more selective about what cuts of meat were to be taken back to South Lake. Any meat that they did

not take could be used by George as he saw fit. By the start of the
third day hunting was less important than bringing in the meat piles
to select and prepare each piece for travel. It was with this in mind
that Eddy and Wellington went over to Foxholm Lake.[6]

One of their meat piles had been disturbed, the covering brush
thrown off and the meat scattered. Birds had gotten at the meat and
it was ruined. There was disagreement between Wellington and Eddy
as to whether or not any of the meat was missing, but there was no
disagreement that the area was full of *bekaycho* tracks. They returned
to the cabins and, after a brief discussion with George, all three armed
themselves and set forth. They took the canoe east along the north
shore of Foxholm Lake, several times leaving it to search inland. Their
pursuit of *bekaycho* was a hunt, one with a declared intent to shoot
*bekaycho* on sight.

Unknown to George and known only in general terms to
Wellington and Eddy, survey teams of the Canadian Archaeological
Service under the direction of Dr. Bryan C. Gordon had used
EtƟen-che's camp as a staging area before dispersing to the various
lakes they were to explore. A two-man team, consisting of a Mr.
Metcalf and a Mr. Morrison, canoed down to cover Foxholm Lake. At
one stage their survey covered the west bay of Foxholm Lake. This
bay, almost a separate lake, is directly north of the cabins George
was using and is in the core of the hunting area the Chipewyan use
while they are living here. George and I later found two of their test
digs on this bay, one of which was the hole first associated with
*bekaycho*, as well as canoe tracks in shallow water and other signs
of their passage.

I met Gordon and Metcalf at the 1976 meetings of the Archaeological Association of the University of Calgary. In the course of that
meeting, Metcalf informed me that Morrison wore size thirteen shoes
and liked to go about barefoot. Aside from a slight concern at the
results had a meeting with the Chipewyan occurred, they were unable
to shed any light on events at Foxholm Lake. Metcalf said he did not
recall seeing piles of meat on the lake and saw no sign the lake was
being used by Indians. I have not met Morrison and cannot confirm
Metcalf's account of his shoe size.[7] Both men seemed astonished when
I related these events to them and again stated their unawareness of
any Chipewyan on Foxholm Lake. When I told them of *bekaycho*'s

mocking cry they feared that it might have been their distant sing-
ing or harmonica playing that was at fault, but that is extremely
unlikely. These northern lakes are prime breeding areas for the common loon (*Gavia immer*) and the source of the mocking cries at dusk
was almost certainly one of these birds displaying part of its enor-
mous vocal repertoire. Loons are not silent in summer as they are in
winter, and their vocalizations when they have young nearby can
sound uncannily human. To hear one call your name from the water
is a most disconcerting experience.

There is no determinable physical explanation for what happened.
The archaeologists denied seeing any meat piles and may not even
have been on the lake when they were disturbed. The sound of rifle
fire carries a long way and certainly the shots fired during the hunting would have alerted anyone nearby to the presence of other
humans. Black bear will throw a meat pile around but they also, so
the Chipewyan say, urinate and defecate on the meat. Grizzly bear
were just returning to the area but after Wellington's embarrassment
with Corky at the hands of a grizzly at South Lake, there was no way
he would have confused grizzly tracks for *bekaycho*.[8] Wolf tracks
are unmistakable. I cannot imagine all three of these experienced
hunters confusing bear, fox, wolverine, or any other animal tracks
with the signs left by *bekaycho*.

Whatever *bekaycho* was, if it was anything, it is perhaps just as
well they did not find it. For it and for them.

The caribou hunting expedition of Wellington and Eddy brought
George and Wellington into cooperation with each other but the
*bekaycho* hunt brought them into participation in the same activity. It is important to realize that it was a hunt they were conducting, one with all the features of the shared expression of Chipewyan
male values that only a hunt can provide. They did not just act as if
they were on a hunt, they *said* they were on a hunt. Years later, they
still say it was a hunt and express thanks that they did not meet
*bekaycho* for fear that they might have gotten into trouble for killing it.[9] To regard this hunt as nothing more than a simple search for
an ordinary stranger, a solution made all the more tempting by the
Chipewyan antipathy to the taking of human life and their knowledge that the archaeologists were in the area is to deny completely
that they had any self-awareness of their actions. When Chipewyan

hunters say that they are on a hunt, I think it pays to listen to them.[10]

Bogeymen may or may not be human; *bekaycho*'s humanity was uncertain, but it does not really matter for a human–nonhuman distinction was not salient here. The hunt was for a shared symbolic construction and whatever *bekaycho* meant to George and Wellington individually, they were able to maintain that symbolic construction and use it as a means of almost ritual interaction in a context where their joint participation was mandatory. The immediate context was so compelling and its consequences to their relations so significant that *bekaycho* became a coercive reality.

The breach between George and Wellington was healed.

1. Canadian law is somewhat paradoxical upon this issue. Little Ann was born nontreaty, gained the status because she was raised by treaty grandparents who formally adopted her, only to loose it again when she married a local nontreaty man.

2. I urge those readers of a more scientific or materialistic bent now gagging on muzzy romanticism to reconsider their reaction. The Chipewyan are different from us in thought, deed, proxemics, and manner. I am no judge of mosquito taste preferences, and the small frogs of the tundra margin may be indifferent to human ethnicity, but from the small predators through the major prey species there is the sensory capacity to react to human differences. To assume that bear and wolf note not between the Old Spice clad, booted constable dressed all in nylon and polyester and the moccasined, fur, cotton, and leather clad *dene* smelling of wood fire and dog team is a Western intellectual and cultural myopia I can no longer fathom.

3. Joan did not believe in feeding her children canned or powdered milk. After they came off the breast their meals consisted largely of several tablespoons of sugar dissolved along with one or two tablespoons of Tang in an eight ounce bottle. When the Tang ran out, Jello or tea were used as substitutes. Their diet was supplemented by other foods but not to a satisfactory level. Joan resisted everyone's efforts to have her change her children's diet.

4. Chipewyan say the black flies all fly to the caribou as they move south.

5. This is a standard practice when a number of men are hunting in the same area. Knowing where other hunters are or the direction they are traveling helps reduce the number of accidental shootings.

6. I do not think George helped. Handling someone else's meat could be construed as making a claim to it, and in this still sensitive atmosphere I think George would have avoided the situation.

7. An undergraduate student in one of my courses who did know him indicated he did not have the size thirteen feet attributed to him.

8. Wellington was determined to erase that memory and pursued every sign of grizzly for two years until he finally found one, faced it, and killed it.

9. When Eddy saw the bogeyman along the road to Mission in 1984, he stopped his truck and asked if assistance was needed. The bogeyman stood without answering

and then turned and ran off into the bush. Virginia had to physically grab hold of Eddy to restrain him from taking his rifle and pursuing.

10. It is a curious image, these three grown men armed to the teeth, prowling the bush with intent to kill a creature none of them "believed" existed. Their behavior confirms Needham's (1972) arguments. An analysis of their actions in terms of our concept of belief would collapse into a projection of meaningless cultural specificity.

# Chapter Nine

The conflict engendered by the clash in the logic of egalitarianism and the birth-ordered locus of authority among siblings had little meaning beyond the context of Wellington's attempt to reconstruct the group around himself. In the course of their maturation George and Wellington had often lived together as well as separately. The potentiality of severed relations between them, preempted by May's passionate reaction to George's departure, is a common and ordinary risk in the life cycle of the conjugal family as its junior members mature. What remained to be decided after May's actions determined that her children would not split apart, were only considerations of pride and emotion; aspects of human life remarkably amenable to symbolic resolution. After the hunt for *bekaycho* George and Wellington did not return to the same affectual state that had preceded their conflict but they did reenter a structured reciprocal relationship within which a positive affectual balance could reassert itself. The definition of this new stage in their relationship as brothers really began in the hunt for *bekaycho*, a hunt that symbolized their new alliance through a mutual celebration of Chipewyan values. This celebration only coincidentaly confirmed the transition of *bekaycho* into the male culture of the Chipewyan.

Beyond the confines of camp or village, hunting is almost a state of being for Chipewyan men, but hunting can be usefully differentiated from a hunt, even when the former involves an encounter with and the actual killing of game. The point of the distinction is a man's deliberate pursuit within the field of *inkoze* of a known prey. Chipewyan often engage in hunting in the company of other men, but a hunt has about it a dual status, being simultaneously a social activity and a solitary one. The shared context of *inkoze* makes a hunt social, but the necessity for the prey to give its consent makes a hunt always in the nature of a solitary examination of each hunter by something beyond the human. The process translates Chipewyan male identity from the abstract to the tangible, and the events of each hunt are then further translated into the social fabric by the verbal recountings that substitute for observation of the actual events by the wider social body. Once the recountings are made to the wider social body, it is that social body that assigns meaning to the events.

As the conflict between George and Wellington developed from the telling of tales to women, to the telling of tales about women, before finally forcing the cessation of normal exchanges of foodstuffs and a modification of relations between women, it was the two men's refusal to share the hunt that first signaled the seriousness of the situation. All the participants were involved in long-term relationships, most were life-long and all of them were fated to continue on for years. After the men's refusal to share the hunt—except for pursuits from camp—their activities were always mediated by a third person to whom they were equally related. The presence of a mediator turned the dyadic relationship into a triadic one that created its own peculiar dynamics. Triads, like other combinations of persons, tend to fall into stable patterns and a triad has among its most stable configurations the alliance of two members against the third.[1]

Because it involves *inkoze*, a hunt is a short-term, temporally bounded activity somewhat removed from normal considerations of time, space, and the effect of past relationships. Each hunt is an episodic relationship within a series of longer-term relationships. The participants come to it with a known history of relationship, but a hunt is more like a pick-up game: a thing of defined duration without a history or a future. The mediating third person, standing always in a relationship of affinity and equality to George and Wellington, was also always in a relationship of a lesser order of closeness than the hierarchical sibling relationship in which they stood to each other. In order for that person to preserve his own position and ability to interact with both of them, he had to exercise a certain judgment and discipline. Any escalation in the conflict between George and Wellington risked the termination of all positive relations between the lot of them. The efforts of the third person to remain neutral created a situation in which each brother was able to perceive himself in a relationship of alliance with his affine, creating a double-false perception of the situation, as each brother perceived himself at the apex of an alliance against his brother. Within each hunt, the affine was seen as an ally without the hunt itself lasting long enough for that affine to have to commit himself to a single brother. The equally related affine is the structurally perfect mediator and has only to avoid taking sides in the presence of both brothers to exercise that function.

All of the major species Chipewyan hunt can be pursued by individual men or by men in collective hunts and still express the particular values that give the hunt its special character. In a normal hunt the prey is a familiar, if uncertain, entity, but *bekaycho* was an atypical prey, a unique form that could produce this sharing of values only in a collective hunt. *Bekaycho* was a being that symbolizes the alien and the unseen, uniting the Chipewyan in segmentary opposition to an external threat. The conflict between Wellington and George became secondary to their shared status of being Chipewyan men.

By no means do all activities of men or relationships between men participate in the special nature of the hunt, but any of their activities and relationships potentially have that peculiar capacity for perpetual measurement that comes from the implicit bedding of male activities in *inkoze*. Close kinship working in conjunction with coresidence can suppress these implicit dynamics of *inkoze*, but that underlying association threatens to assert itself at any disruption of the suppressing mechanisms. This gives a fundamentally different conceptual nature to relationships between men than is found in relationships between women. Of necessity, the expression of power in interpersonal relationships varies as a function of the applicability of *inkoze* to the relationships, yet the metaphors of power, as with the geographical metaphors considered earlier, operate for both genders despite the different conceptual base upon which the actions of men and women are ordered.

May's display of passion, fear, and hurt when George and his family departed for Foxholm Lake was an exercise of power that seems to rest purely upon the use of affectual ties, but the power of sentiment[2] she used so effectively was not an inherent product of her role as mother. "Mother" is only a kinship term, a word that is associated with a variety of individuals and values that can be used to create sentimental ties to various people, including biological children. One is not a mother as a product of reproduction or natural sentimental ties but through the use of certain culturally ordered forms of behavior that (sometimes) result in the development of certain patterns of sentiment. May's use of sentiment to bind her family around her was equally dependent upon Chipewyan ideas of marriage and authority that were far removed from ideas of motherhood and lacking perception in terms of *inkoze*. May's relationships to her children, both male and female, lacked entirely the structured competitive base that at least implicitly underlay the relationships between Paul and his sons.

Paul was in a position to try to prevent George from leaving although he chose not to do so. Like him, May lacked the authority to determine the behavior of her adult sons, but she was also unable even to make a credible attempt at dissuading George from leaving. She could speak and be heard, but the underlying logic of *inkoze* in male to male relationships meant that her words would be discounted. Her use of anger to redefine the situation after George departed accomplished that redefinition through the manipulation of ideas of family, kinship, and classification rather than through the manipulation of sentiment. As was the case with the reactions of the women toward *bekaycho*, the issue here is beyond explanation in terms of rationality. Affect/emotion/sensation provide more than an aesthetic for rational thought, they provide an ordered mode of thought independent of verbal capabilities.

Faced with the possibility of a permanent fission of her family, May directed her anger at Paul and made the confrontation occur at individual personality to individual personality level. The intensity of the conflict raised the spectre of fission at the more basic categorical level of the conjugal tie between her and Paul. She inverted the threat to her family posed by her sons' actions by threatening to drive away their father. That relationship had served as the point by which all of her children had defined their own relationships to each other. This forced all her children at the camp to recognize that their own actions could result in the disintegration of their whole kin group.

Wellington, who was the real focus of May's concern, was outmaneuvered even before he realized there was a contest. May had no intention of leaving Paul, and George was not even there to witness her outburst, but that was of no consequence in the generated solidarity of the existing categorical kin relations. Her skilled expressive performance was not based upon the allocation of the sentiment–structure dichotomy in the mother–father roles but drew upon that aspect of the Chipewyan conceptualization and construction of gender roles that equates female with non-*inkoze* in the classification and interpretation of the causal base and significance of women's actions.


After they returned to South Lake, Wellington, Eddy, and little Ann (who came with them) all gave their own versions of the events at Foxholm Lake. On the basis of those stories there emerged a consensus that *bekaycho* was tall, not very heavy, and wore shoes rather than boots. The description and interpretation of the tracks *bekaycho* left around the lake were the main evidence upon which this conclusion was based. Wellington and Eddy said that George had been thinking about moving his family to an island,[3] but as we were soon to move to Foxholm Lake, no one seemed very worried about him. There was really very little talk of *bekaycho*. The women and older children thought George had seen signs left by the archaeologists and was rather foolish to have mistaken them for signs of *bekaycho*. The pending departure of Virginia and Eddy and our own move to Foxholm Lake were the prevalent topics of discussion.

Virginia and Eddy's plane arrived on August 11, and we moved to Foxholm Lake the same day. Paul and I left last, my canoe strapped onto the float of the aircraft. The pilot flew us just to the river–lake chain, and I could see part of the route along which George, and later Eddy and Wellington, had traveled.[4] We reached the cabins late that night.

Our arrival at Foxholm Lake found George improving physically and ready for company, but there was no talk of *bekaycho*. In the next three-and-a-half months *bekaycho* was mentioned only four times that I know of: when George showed me the tracks and test dig on the bay of Foxholm Lake; on August 19, when we found the archaeologists' canoe tracks on a distant part of the lake; and on our early September canoe trip to EtƟen-che's when we passed the spot where he had heard *bekaycho*'s mocking cry. George had accepted the archaeologists as *bekaycho* and was miffed by their rudeness in moving the meat piles. He in no way indicated that he regarded *bekaycho* as anything other than ordinary humans.

The final time was late in the fall, and I brought up the topic. The fall was a hard one. Few caribou came after early September and most of the meat piles that had been made fell prey to a small black bear of prodigious appetite. The weather stayed warm, delaying freeze-up until late October and creating difficult travel conditions and poor hunting. The camp was often hungry, our only fresh meat coming from a lucky late kill of some rutting bulls. I wondered if the stress might reactivate George's interest in *bekaycho* and raised the subject with him. He was willing to talk about it with me but showed little interest in it. The ease with which *bekaycho*, a creature that had so recently motivated their actions, could be dismissed showed its primacy as social fiction over any issue of its explanation or reality.

Jean and Miley joined Wellington in the fall and remained at his camp until Christmas, 1975. Miley and Wellington came to Foxholm Lake for a visit on October 17, well before the lake ice was suited for safe travel. Wellington crossed a narrow neck of ice to get to camp but Miley refused to cross. We spent an amusing hour sitting with Paul and May's cabin door open, listening to him curse his dogs as he struggled around a safer overland route. There was no mention of *bekaycho* during their visit.

I returned to the field in the summer of 1977, and spent several months at Foxholm Lake. We set our tents on the sand point where George first encountered the tracks of *bekaycho*. The tracks were gone but it was still possible to see the test digs and to find other traces of the archaeologists. The breach between Wellington and George had remained healed. They were not demonstrably close in affect but they did cooperate and assist each other as they moved through their separate cycles of activity.

George told a version of what had happened here in 1975, a version based upon a near encounter with the archaeologists. Virginia, little Ann, and Barb retained an interest in Bigfoot and Virginia had several times requested that we send her information about Bigfoot. That interest had faded by 1978. By then the cumulative effects of small changes over the last decade were generating some substantial shifts in the economic patterns and social organization of Mission. *Bekaycho* was largely lost in these changes. For most of the people in camp that spring and summer of 1975, *bekaycho* had become a referential shorthand for the troubles between George and Wellington. The Chipewyan still prefer to date things by events and it was *bekaycho* that they had chosen to date that period.

Before I returned to mission in 1983, I wrote, "I cannot predict the success of *bekaycho* in establishing itself in the verbal culture of the Mission Chipewyan generally. Among this one set of extended kin it is firmly established as a minor variant of the bogeyman motif and will be carried on by these people in this form. If it spreads through their entire network of close kin and affines and to the growing children of the participants, *bekaycho* will have spread to nearly 10 percent of the village population. This does not seem an adequate base for it, without some other input from English-speaking culture, to become a general feature of the culture, but it is also too large a percentage for it to be lost."

In that short summer visit of 1983, I spoke with George, May, and Paul about these events and talked with Eddy in passing. Wellington had already left for the bush by the time I arrived, and I did not get a chance to talk with him. Mickey and Mike had been too young in 1975, to remember those events in 1983. *Bekaycho* does not seem to be spreading to the children of the group.

When I mentioned *bekaycho* to May, she began immediately to talk about it. She remembered the events clearly, but *bekaycho* had become irrelevant. What she remembered, and talked about, was the trouble between her sons. We talked about that topic at length and her use of *bekaycho* was twofold: as a shorthand reference to date that time and its events, and as a means of expressing the different natures and personalities of these middle two of her sons. She regards Wellington and George as friends but not as being friendly. They do camp together but only when she and Paul are with them. May said Wellington was too concerned with material goods. She pointed to the house in which he now lived, boarded up for his season in the bush, and said she "didn't know how much stuff he had in there, that he never threw anything away." She speculated that even the first kicker (outboard motor) that his father had ever used, way back in the 1930s, was somewhere in there. I asked if Wellington was trying to gain control of people that time in 1975, trying to be the "boss." She said, "That is the way he is." She spoke of George differently, saying, "You only have to tell him something and right away he believes."[5] Her use of *bekaycho* was as a code for family history and relations between family members.

May attributed to little Ann a related version of some of the events that she herself had not seen. The cry mocking the baby that George heard after they were resupplied was said to be nothing but an echo of the baby crying.[6] It was from this version that I learned of the loose dog that delayed their entry to the cabins. Little Ann still did not know of the connection George had made between the dog's noises and the Old Black Woman's death. May was not impressed by the connection when I told her of it.

Little Ann's story, and May's comments upon it, focus on George's gullibility for accepting so readily something like *bekaycho*. There are details in little Ann's version, like the presence of a high wind, that were not in George's first accounts but that were in his versions of 1977 and 1983. May insisted that, from the time it happened, little Ann had insisted that the mocking cry was only an echo. Little Ann was only eleven in 1975, and I cannot be certain just how much of the story was hers and and how much was May's.

The way in which little Ann and May attribute gullibility to George for accepting the reality of *bekaycho* contrasts with their own behavior and words at the time the events happened. George was the man most prone of all the men to accept *bekaycho*, but he was far less ready to do so than were the women and children themselves. I was not there long enough to determine if the charge of gullibility was related to a man accepting something that his gender should have led him not to accept or if there has been a change in the pattern by which all Chipewyan accept something like *bekaycho*.

If *bekaycho* has a social referent for May and little Ann, it also has a geographical referent for George and Joan. For personal and aesthetic reasons, George prefers to base himself near Foxholm Lake and for him *bekaycho* is tied to that locale. He will pass on to his children the stories of *bekaycho* as part of the lore of the place. Reference of *bekaycho* to South Lake is temporarily moot, as they have abandoned camping on that lake. If they should return there, *bekaycho* may resurface as part of its history.

The version George told in 1983 is a bit more interesting than the one he told in 1977. The refined version carries on the main events in a more polished form, reflecting further time for elaboration and transformation. It might also reflect a greater willingness to talk about the events. In 1983, we were in the village and eight years removed from those events, whereas in 1977, we were on the actual site where they happened and only two years removed from them in time. He now begins his story with the landing of the aircraft that brought him his supplies. On this plane are an RCMP constable, the pilot, one of the chiefs, Paul, and an unknown Indian affairs man.[7] He breaks from these events to tell how earlier in the day he had missed a shot at a caribou on one of the portages. The caribou was standing on a small ridge and the shot went high, carrying over the ridge and a startled archaeologist on the other side. The archaeologist remained out of sight and followed them, either provoked or frightened by the incident. George was not sure what the motivation was, but was convinced he saw the archaeologist on the return trip as the skulking figure in the dark. He insists that the mocking noise was not that of an animal, a bird, or of an echo. That *bekaycho* was the archaeologist[8] is firmly established in his own mind, and he still insists that he was ready to shoot him on sight. *Bekaycho* did disturb his meat pile and removed ribs and tenderloin strips from Wellington and Eddy's cache.[9] The barefoot aspect of Morrison's 1976 statements is absent from George's stories. *Bekaycho* now wears "work shoes, with low tops."

The readiness with which these events were recalled and discussed after eight years shows that they have not been reduced to insignificance. The people required no prompting to talk about them and they all had an excellent recall of the details. Poking fun at George is the most common justification the women give to tell the stories and parallels the way they talked of Joan's manipulation of George's notions of pollution. If making fun of George is the idiom, it remains that these stories are a shorthand for the period of adjustment between George and Wellington. The nature of the relationship between these two men can be conveyed without having to raise the topic directly or repeat the old allegations. I would not go so far as to say that a person asking about the history of relations between these two men, if any one would do such a thing, would be told these stories, but younger family members hearing them would know enough of the context of family history to understand.

George has recast the Bigfoot entirely. What began as a story told by a white fisherman was transformed initially by Wellington into a variant of the bogeyman pattern. George has created from that version and his own experience a classic bogeyman encounter: a renegade white man lurking around a camp for no discernible purpose. *Bekaycho* was a threat to the women and children, it stole meat, it violated a cache, and it wasted caribou. Its presence and its antisocial nature were known only through these secretive actions. The transformation of Bigfoot to *bekaycho* into bogeyman is complete right down to the footprints of its hard-soled shoes.

The nature of this small group's exposure to Bigfoot and the particular characteristics of this Western symbolic form were part of the reason it made a successful transition between the two cultures, but they were not in and of themselves very significant factors in its adoption. We must look to the Chipewyan practice of marking time by events, the nature of power in the society, and the nature of the conceptualization and construction of gender in Chipewyan culture to understand the reason for Bigfoot's transformation into *bekaycho*.

The first issue requires the least discussion but was the one most in need of the passage of time to determine. Not until the summer of 1983 could I be sure that these events would be remembered and see that they had become a shorthand for the events of 1975. The ability of this group of people to transform the motif and then use it as a means of allusion to things best not plainly talked about indicates that *bekaycho* had been made consonant with other culturally patterned modes of storing information. The Chipewyan might have been able to know this in 1975 but I was not able to do so. The mode of storing information that Bigfoot became was related to the manner in which they express power. Chipewyan do not like direct expressions of power and most particularly do not like them among kin. Creating from Bigfoot something that could be used as a means of allusion to unpleasant negotiations of power and encoding family history gave *bekaycho* both immediate and long-term utility.

From the beginning I have chosen not to focus upon women. Gender is strongly marked in Chipewyan society, but it is not a male–female distinction that is operative here but an adult male–everyone else distinction. The reason for not focusing on everyone else hangs on three points: (1) the reality of bogeymen, (2) symbolic male control of women and children, and (3) the competitive logic of *inkoze*. Men, women, and children, do not live in precisely the same world. For women and children the bogeyman is a real and present threat. This is not an issue of different beliefs with some implied notion of confusion or misperception, but is in fact an accurate perception of the different physical and social environments in which they live. There may not be very many bogeymen "out there" but there are some of them out there and their target is women and children. Surely the transition from child to adult male is partly marked by changes in how a boy reacts to the bogeyman. We may choose to regard the threat of bogeymen as too improbable to take seriously, we may continue to regard them only as creatures of legend or projective psychological disorder, but when the women and children of this camp chose to take *bekaycho* seriously they were responding to a set of known and real threats and were taking stock of new information about a source of physical danger.

Recognizing that men, women, and children live in different worlds at the level of "reality" as well as in the reality of symbolism is a, however obvious and minor, key to the interpretation of social systems that may be problematic if we assume culture to be a single monolithic social and symbolic construction. Symbols and symbolic forms do not create uniformity of meaning at the individual level but only the illusion of uniformity. That each individual makes shades of association different from those made by others is suitably camouflaged in most situations from participant and observer alike, but this is not always the case. The transformation of Bigfoot into *bekaycho* among the women and children of this Chipewyan grouping was a process that reflected the "real world" within which they happen to live. This was not the case with the men.

The major relevant factor in how males conceptualize bogeymen is their shared understanding that men do not fear or worry about bogeymen. The explanation of the transformation of Bigfoot to *bekaycho* and their use of *bekaycho* depends upon the realization that they were able to do so precisely when they could replicate the general pattern of use of bogeymen as a form of social fiction in their hunt for *bekaycho*. Only when this was done did the form become socially useful and fixed among them as a feature of their relationships to each other. Before that point, even for George, the form was but a trivial part of the way in which they related to women and children. I do not mean to denigrate the fact of that use, for it was an aspect of how they maintained control over those women and children (and vice versa), but something was added when they were able to use it among themselves without reference to the women and children.

The transformation of Bigfoot to *bekaycho* among this small party of Chipewyan in one sense confirms the advantage of seeking to understand symbols only through their relation to other symbols, but it also indicates some of the limits of that approach. To examine symbols only in their relation to other symbols is to avoid questions of both belief and social practice. Can symbols be profitably examined by assuming belief? If we retain the concept of belief as a means of explaining the actions of people in other cultures, then we risk complicating our analyses for we must also then assume that to believe and to not believe are equally powerful and normal means by which symbols operate and are transmitted. Chipewyan culture uses what our culture calls belief simultaneously with nonbelief on the same symbols and does so according to other systematically distributed variables like age and gender. It is far more parsimonious to dispense with belief and its associated presuppositions and focus less upon the formalization of some dogma and more upon the actual use of symbolic forms in social practice.

1. Levi-Strauss (1955) has provided ample anthropological evidence of the inherently triadic nature of the dyad and the ability of peoples to express dyads in triads. I am, however, drawing upon ideas in social psychology conventionally attributed to Heider (1958). I was first exposed to these ideas from this source and find their earlier formulations and extensions of more utility to my concerns as an ethnographer than I do their later development. T. O. Beidelman has informed me that he regards attribution of credit for these ideas to Heider as an error and that the credit should go to Georg Simmel.

2. The association of sentiment with female, and structure with male, particularly to the roles mother or father, is well established in Northern Athapaskan studies. To accept this dichotomy as it stands is to fall into an extensionist argument about the generation of kinship relationships and terminology.

3. He didn't.

4. The pilot put down in the middle of a long lake on a clear day in bright sunshine and we loaded the canoe from the float. It is easy to create an image of the crystal indigo surface shimmering with the reflected greens, greys, and golds of bounding forest and tundra-swathed hills under a flawless sun, but the lake itself is beyond my power. Translucent blue does not begin to convey how light seems to radiate from the depths and shallows of the lake itself, the whole body of water amplifying the passing sun's light in a diaphanous crystalline haze.

5. Speaking English forces the Chipewyan to make the distinction between belief and nonbelief.

6. George and I passed through this area on our way back from EtΘen-che's camp in September 1975. It is open ground, but this explanation is not without some plausibility. George was carrying the canoe inverted with his head and shoulders inside, and it might have acted as an echo chamber.

7. I did not log all the comings and goings and Paul may well have been along on the flight. I cannot explain the omission of Wellington.

8. He takes no account of there being two archaeologists in the party.

9. In 1983 Eddy still held firm to the disturbance of the meat pile, but he was no longer absolutely certain that meat had been taken from it.

# Epilogue

When I visited Paul and May in 1983 they were raising another small grandchild, this one from a broken marriage of Phil's. For the past several years they had been unable to spend time in the Northwest Territories. The progression of Paul's emphysema had left him semiinvalid. By dint of sheer will he convinced his family he was going to go north at the end of the summer of 1983. They accommodated him, and Paul and May spent several pleasant weeks among the caribou before they returned to the village. They had recently begun to receive old-age pension payments from the Canadian government and were enjoying the highest material standard of living they had ever known. As the snow began to fall in mid-September 1985, Paul died. He was buried in the cemetery near the village.

Mike is now in his midteens, living at home and facing all the problems and trauma normal to teenagers. In the summer of 1984, during the Michael Jackson craze, he bandaged his hand with white tape in imitation of the singer. May and Virginia, upon seeing his hand, rushed to him frantically asking how he had cut himself. Mortified, Mike fled the house leaving it to little Ann to explain the situation to them.

Mickey, last seen climbing on the plane in June of 1975, has married and become a father. He and his wife and infant share May's home. While I was there in 1983, Mickey got his grandmother to watch the baby so he and his wife could go to a friend's house and watch a videotape of a soft-core porn movie. I asked what his prudish grandmother thought of movies like that. He thought a moment and then responded, "I don't think she knows about them."

George and Joan's life has undergone a series of changes. Joan's father died and her mother was unwilling to return to bush life where she would be a dependent in another household. They stayed close to town to be near her, but since an accident left their last-born infant comatose, they have only rarely left town. George has flourished in his new town life, opening a small store, and being recently elected to the council of chiefs.

Wellington has been able to earn an income in the bush for several years, so he and his family spend little time in town. He has steadily accumulated the material things he wanted and his domestic life has finally become the steadying influence of which he was in need. As he is now in his early forties, his sons are old enough to share much of the work with him. Ann's life has been more stable and enjoyable since they have come to spend most of the year away from the problems of the village. As this book prepares to go to press, Wellington has just learned that a sample of good rock that he sent out to be assayed is rich in uranium, gold, and other metals. He is awaiting the melting of the snow in May, at which time a party from the Northwest Territories will assist him in staking claims and determining if the deposit is rich enough to be worked.

Jean has aged greatly and is now largely confined to the village. She remains active but is unable to endure the rigors of bush life without more help than she receives from her sons. Miley and his brother quickly squandered their share of the inheritance. The most interesting recent event in their lives came when a woman whose husband was frequently absent from Mission took a fancy to Miley. His discovery of sex and the enthusiasm with which he pursued his discovery provided the village with weeks of delighted gossip.

Both little Ann and Barb have grown up and married. Little Ann married first and has had two children. Barb became engaged to a teacher in June 1983 and was married the following summer.

Eddy and Virginia continued much as before. She is steadily upgrading her teaching qualifications and still works as a teacher in the school at the administrative center. Eddy had taken employment at a mine and had worked there for several years by the summer of 1983. They have had one more child.

I learned of Corky from Wellington. Corky was arrested some years after 1977, apparently charged with arson for a suspicious fire at one of his outlets. When released, he returned home, took a gun, and shot his wife. He then turned the weapon upon himself fatally. His wife survived and their child was unharmed.

# Bibliography

Asch, M. I. 1981. "Slavey." In *Subarctic*. Vol. 6, ed. J. Helm, 338–349. *Handbook of North American Indians*. Washington, D.C.: Smithsonian Institution Press.

Banfield, A. W. F. 1961. *A Revision of the Reindeer and Caribou, Genus Rangifer*. National Museum of Canada Bulletin no. 177, Biological Series no. 66. Ottawa: Department of Northern Affairs and Natural Resources.

Basso, E. 1978. "The Enemy of Every Tribe: 'Bushman' Images in Northern Athapaskan Narratives." *American Anthropologist* 5 (4): 690–709.

Beidleman, T. O. 1961. "Hyena and Rabbit: A Kaguru Representation of Matrilineal Relations." *Africa* 31:250–257.

———. 1963. "Further Adventures of Hyena and Rabbit: The Folktale as a Sociological Model." *Africa* 33:54–69.

———. 1968. "Some Nuer Notions of nakedness, nudity, and sexuality." *Africa* 38:113–131.

———. 1971. "Kaguru Symbolic Classification." In *Right and Left: Essays on Dual Symbolic Classification*, ed. R. Needham, 128–166. Chicago: University of Chicago Press.

Bishop, C. A. and Kretch, S., III. 1980. "Matriorganization: The Basis of Aboriginal Subarctic Social Organization." *Arctic Anthropology* 17 (2): 34–45.

Brody, H. 1983. *Maps And Dreams: Indians and the British Columbia Frontier*. Bungay, Suffolk: Pelican.

Burch, E. S., Jr. 1972. "The Caribou/Wild Reindeer as a Human Resource." *American Antiquity* 37 (3): 339–368.

———. 1977. "Muskox and Man in the Central Canadian Subarctic 1689–1974." *Arctic* 30:135–154.

Chang, K. C. 1962. "A Typology of Settlement and Community Patterns, in Some Circumpolar Societies." *Arctic Anthropology* 1:28–41.

Clark, A. M. 1981. "Koyukon." In *Subarctic*. Vol. 6, ed. J. Helm, 585–601. *Handbook of North American Indians*. Washington, D.C.: Smithsonian Institution Press.

Cohen, A. 1974. *Two-Dimensional Man*. Berkeley: University of California Press.

Coles, T. L. 1980. "Stanner and Mutjingga: A Reinterpretation of Myth." Master's thesis, department of sociology and anthropology, Simon Fraser University, Burnaby, British Columbia.

Crow, J. and Obley, P. 1981. "Han." In *Subarctic*. Vol. 6, ed. J. Helm, 506–513. *Handbook of North American Indians*. Washington, D.C.: Smithsonian Institution Press.

de Heusch, L. 1985. *Sacrifice in Africa: A Structuralist Approach*. Bloomington, Indiana: Indiana University Press.

de Laguna, F., and McClellan, C. 1981. "Ahtna." In *Subarctic*. Vol. 6, ed. J. Helm, 641–663. *Handbook of North American Indians*. Washington, D.C.: Smithsonian Institution Press.

Douglas, M. T. 1966. *Purity and Danger: An Analysis of the Concepts of Pollution and Taboo*. London: Routledge and Kegan Paul.

Dumont, L. 1983. *Affinity as a Value: Marriage Alliance in South India, with Comparative Essays on Australia*. Chicago: University of Chicago Press.

Durkheim, E. [1915] 1965. *The Elementary Forms of the Religious Life*. Reprint. New York: The Free Press.

Durkheim, E. and Mauss, M. [1903] 1963. *Primitive Classification*. Reprint, trans. R. Needham. Chicago: University of Chicago Press.

Dyck, N. 1980. "Booze, Barrooms and Scrapping: Masculinity and Violence in a Western Canadian Town." *Canadian Journal of Anthropology* 1(2): 191–198.

Dyen, I., and Aberle, D. 1974. *Lexical Reconstruction: The Case of the Proto-Athapaskan Kinship System*. New York: Cambridge University Press.

Firth, R. 1985. "Degrees of Intelligibility." In *Reason and Morality*, ed. J. Overing, 29–46. New York: Tavistock.

Fortune, R. F. 1932. *Sorcerers of Dobu*. New York: E. P. Dutton and Co.

———. 1936. *Manus Religion*. Reprint. Lincoln, Nebraska: University of Nebraska Press.

Foucault, M. 1979. *Discipline and Punish: The Birth of the Prison*. New York: Vintage.

———. 1980. *The History of Sexuality*. Vol. 1. New York: Vintage.

Evans-Pritchard, E. E. 1940. *The Nuer*. Oxford: Clarendon Press.

———. 1956. *Nuer Religion*. New York: Oxford University Press.

Feeley-Harnik, G. 1981. *The Lord's Table: Eucharist and Passover in Early Christianity*. Philadelphia: University of Pennsylvania Press.

Fortes, M., and Evans-Pritchard, E. E. [1940] 1970. "Introduction." In *African Political Systems*. Reprint. Oxford: Oxford University Press.

Gillespie, B. C. 1975. "Territorial Expansion of the Chipewyan in the 18th Century." In Proceedings: Northern Athapaskan Conference, 1971. National Museum of Man, Mercury Series. Canadian Ethnology Service, Paper no. 27: 350–388. Ottawa: National Museums of Canada.

———. 1976. "Changes in Territory and Technology of the Chipewyan." *Arctic Anthropology* 13(1): 6–11.

———. 1981. "Mountain Indians." In *Subarctic*. Vol. 6, ed. J. Helm, 326–337. *Handbook of North American Indians*. Washington, D.C.: Smithsonian Institution Press.

Gould, S. J. 1977. *Ever Since Darwin: Reflections in Natural History*. New York: W. W. Norton and Co.

Hara, S. H. 1980. *The Hare Indians and Their World*. National Museum of Man, Mercury Series. Canadian Ethnology Service, Paper No. 63. Ottawa: National Museums of Canada.

Hearne, S. 1971. *A Journey from Prince of Wales Fort in Hudson's Bay to the Northern Ocean*. Edmonton: M. G. Hurtig, Ltd.

Heider, F. 1958. *The Psychology of Interpersonal Relations*. New York: Wiley.

Helm, J. 1961. *The Lynx Point People: The Dynamics Of A Northern Athapaskan Band*. National Museums of Canada, Bulletin no. 176, Anthropological Series no. 53. Ottawa: Department of Northern Affairs and National Resources.

———. 1968. "The Nature of Dogrib Socio-Territorial Groups." In *Man The Hunter*, eds. Lee, R., and Devore, I. 118–125. Chicago: Aldine.

———. 1981. *Subarctic*. Vol. 6. *Handbook of North American Indians*. Washington, D.C.: Smithsonian Institution Press.

Helm, J.; Alliband, T.; Birk, T.; Lawson, V.; Reisner, S.; Sturtevant, C.; and Witkowski, S. 1975. "The Contact History of the Subarctic Athapaskans: An Overview." In *Proceedings: Northern Athapaskan Conference, 1971*, Vol. I, ed. A. M. Clark, 302–349. National Museum of Man, Mercury series. Canadian Ethnology Service, Paper no. 27. Ottawa: National Museums of Canada.

Helm, J., and Damas, D. 1963. "The Contact-Traditional All-Native Community of the Canadian North: The Upper Mackenzie 'Bush' Athapaskans and the Igluligmiut." *Anthropologica*. n.s. 5:9–22.

Hobart, M. 1985. "Anthropos Through the Looking-glass: Or How to Teach the Balinese to Bark." In *Reason and Morality*, ed J. Overing, 104–134. New York: Tavistock.

Honigmann, J. 1981. "Kaska." In *Subarctic*. Vol. 6, ed. J. Helm, 442–450. *Handbook of North American Indians*. Washington, D.C.: Smithsonian Institution Press.

Huber, P. B. 1980. "The Anggor Bowman: Ritual and Society in Melanesia." *American Ethnologist.* 7(1): 43–57.

Huntington, W. R. 1973. *Religion and Social Organization of the Bara People of Madagascar.* Ann Arbor, Michigan: University Microfilms.

Ingold, T. 1983. "The Significance of Storage in Hunting Societies." *Man* n.s. 18(3): 553–571.

Irimoto, T. 1981. *Chipewyan Ecology: Group Structure and Caribou Hunting System.* Senri Ethnological Studies no. 8. Osaka: National Museum of Ethnology.

Jarvenpa, R. 1976. "Spatial and Ecological Factors in the Annual Economic Cycle of the English River Band of Chipewyan." *Arctic Anthropology* n.s. 18(1) 45–60.

———. 1977. "The Ubiquitous Bushman: Chipewyan–White Trapper Relations of the 1930s." In *Prehistory of the North American Subarctic: The Athapaskan Question.* Proceedings of the Ninth Annual Conference. Calgary: The Archaeological Association of the University of Calgary.

———. 1982. "Intergroup Behavior and Imagery: The Case of Chipewyan and Cree." *Ethnology* 31(4): 283-299.

Kenny, M. G. 1981. "Mirror in the Forest: The Dorobo Hunter-Gatherers as an Image of the Other." *Africa* 51(1): 477– 495.

———. 1982. "The Stranger from the Lake: A Theme in the History of the Lake Victoria Shorelands." *Azania* 17:1– 26.

Koolage, W. W. 1975. "Conceptual Negativism in Chipewyan Ethnology." *Anthropologica* n.s. 18(1): 45–60.

Layton, R. 1986. "Political and Territorial Structures among Hunter-Gatherers." *Man* n.s. 2(1): 18–33.

Leach, E. 1966. *Rethinking Anthropology.* London: Athlone Press.

Levi-Strauss, C.L. 1955. "Social Structures of Central and Eastern Brazil." Chapter 6: 116–127 and "Do Dual Organizations Exist?" Chapter 7: 128–160. In *Structural Anthropology.* Garden City, N.J.: Anchor.

———. 1967. "The Story Of Asdiwal." In *The Structural Study of Myth and Totemism,* ed. E. Leach. London: Tavistock.

———. 1969. *The Elementary Structures of Kinship.* London: Eyre and Spottiswoode.

———. 1981. *The Naked Man.* New York: Harper and Row.

Levy-Bruhl, L. [1923] 1967. *Primitive Mentality.* Reprint. Boston: Beacon Press.

———. [1926] 1979. *How Natives Think.* Reprint. New York: Arno Press.

Lowie, R. 1912. "Chipewyan Tales." *Anthropological Papers of the American Museum of Natural History* 10:171–200.

_____. 1925. "Windigo: A Chipewyan Story." In *American Indian Life*, ed. E. C. Parsons, 325–336. New York.

MacLachlan, B. 1981. "Tahltan." In *Subarctic*. Vol. 6, ed. J. Helm, 458–468. *Handbook of North American Indians*. Washington, D.C.: Smithsonian Institution Press.

McClellan, C. 1981. "Tutchone." In *Subarctic*. Vol. 6, ed. J. Helm, 493–505. *Handbook of North American Indians*. Washington, D.C.: Smithsonian Institution Press.

Mauss. M. [1925] 1967. *The Gift*. Reprint. New York: W. W. Norton and Co. Inc.

Morgan, L. H. [1878] 1964. *Ancient Society*. Reprint, ed. L.A. White. Cambridge: Belknap, Harvard University Press.

Needham, R. 1962. *Structure And Sentiment*. Chicago: University of Chicago Press.

_____. 1966. "Age, Category, and Descent." *Bijdragen tot des Tall-, Land, En Volkenkunde* n.p. 2:1–35.

_____. 1972. *Belief, Language, and Experience*. Oxford: Basil Blackwell.

_____. 1974. *Remarks & Inventions: Skeptical Essays About Kinship*. London: Tavistock.

_____. 1975. "Polythetic Classification: Convergence and Consequences." *Man* n.s. 10:349–369.

_____. 1978. *Primordial Characters*. Charlottesville, Va.: University of Virginia Press.

_____. 1979. *Symbolic Classification*. Santa Monica, California: Goodyear Publishing Co.

_____. 1980. *Reconnaissances*. Toronto: University of Toronto.

O'Keefe, D. L. 1983. *Stolen Lightning: The Social Theory Of Magic*. New York: Random House.

Osgood, C. B. 1933. *The Ethnography of the Great Bear Lake Indians*. (from the annual report, 1931,). Ottawa: National Museums of Canada.

Overing, J. 1985. *Reason And Morality*. New York: Tavistock.

Parkin, D. 1985. "Reason, Emotion, and the Embodiment of Power." In *Reason and Morality*, ed. J. Overing, 135–151. New York: Tavistock.

Ridington, R. 1968. "The Medicine Fight: An Instrument of Political Process Among the Beaver Indians." *American Anthropologist*. 70(6): 1152–1160.

_____. 1981. "Beaver." In *Subarctic*. Vol. 6, ed. J. Helm, 350–360. *Handbook of North American Indians*. Washington, D.C.: Smithsonian Institution Press.

Sansom, B. 1980. *The Camp at Wallaby Cross*. Canberra: Australian Institute of Aboriginal Studies.

Savishinsky, J. 1975. "The Dog & the Hare: Canine Culture in an Athapaskan Band." In *Proceedings: Northern Athapaskan Conference, 1971.* National Museum of Man, Mercury Series, Canadian Ethnology Service, Paper no. 27(2)462–515. Ottawa: National Museums of Canada.

Savishinsky, J., and Hara, H. 1981. "Hare." In *Subarctic.* Vol. 6, ed. J. Helm, 314–325. *Handbook of North American Indians.* Washington, D.C.: Smithsonian Institution Press.

Seton, E. T. [1911] 1981. *The Arctic Prairies.* Reprint. Toronto: Fitzhenry and Whiteside, Ltd.

Service, E. 1962. *Primitive Social Organization.* New York: Random House.

Slobodin, R. 1960. "Some Social Functions of Kutchin Anxiety." *American Anthropologist* 62(1): 122–133.

_____. 1962. *Band Organization of the Peel River Kutchin.* National Museums of Canada, Bulletin no. 179. Ottawa: National Museums of Canada.

_____. 1969. "Leadership and Participation in a Kutchin Trapping Party." In *Contributions To Anthropology: Band Societies,* ed. D. Damas, 56–89. Anthropological Series 84, National Museum Of Canada, Bulletin 228. Ottawa: National Museums of Canada.

_____. 1970. "Kutchin Concepts of Reincarnation." *Western Canadian Journal Of Anthropology* 2(1): 67–79.

_____. 1975. "Without Fire: A Kutchin Tale of Warfare, Survival, and Vengeance." In *Proceedings: Northern Athapaskan Conference, 1971,* Vol. 1:259–301. National Museum of Man, Mercury Series. Canadian Ethnology Service, Paper no. 27. Ottawa: National Museums of Canada.

Smith, D. M. 1973. *Inkonze: Magico-Religious Beliefs of Contact-Traditional Chipewyan Trading at Fort Resolution, NWT, Canada.* National Museum of Man, Mercury Series. Ethnology Division Paper No. 6. Ottawa: National Museums of Canada.

_____. 1982. *Moose-Deer Island House People: A History of the Native People of Fort Resolution.* National Museum of Man, Mercury Series. Canadian Ethnology Service, Paper no. 81. Ottawa: National Museums Of Canada.

_____. 1985. "Big Stone Foundations: Manifest Meaning in Chipewyan Myths." *Journal Of American Culture* 18(1): 73–77.

Smith, J. G. E. 1970. "The Chipewyan Hunting Group in a Village Context." *Western Canadian Journal of Anthropology* 2(1): 60–66.

_____. 1975. "The Ecological Basis of Chipewyan Socio-Territorial Organization." In *Proceedings: Northern Athapaskan Conference, 1971.*

National Museum of Man, Mercury Series. Canadian Ethnology Service, Paper no. 27: 389– 461. Ottawa: National Museums of Canada.

_____. 1976. "Local Band Organization of the Caribou-Eater Chipewyan." *Arctic Anthropology* 13 (1): 12–24.

_____. 1978. "The Emergence of the Micro-Urban Village Among the Caribou-Eater Chipewyan." *Human Organization* 37 (1): 38–49.

_____. 1981. "Chipewyan." In *Subarctic.* Vol. 6, ed J. Helm, 271-284. *Handbook of North American Indians.* Washington, D.C.: Smithsonian Institution Press.

_____. n.d. Personal communications.

Smith, J. G. E. and Burch, E. S., Jr. 1979. "Chipewyan and Inuit in the Central Canadian Subarctic, 1613–1977." *Arctic Anthropology* 16(2): 76–101.

Stanner, W. E. H. 1963. *On Aboriginal Religion.* Oceania Monograph Series no. 11. Sidney: Oceania.

_____. 1965a. "Durmugan, A Nangiomeri." In *In The Company Of Men,* ed. J. B. Casagrande, New York: Harper Torchbooks.

_____. 1965b. "The Dreaming." In *Reader In Comparative Religion,* eds. W. Lessa and E. Vogt, 158–167. New York: Harper and Row.

Steward, J. 1955. *Theory Of Culture Change: The Methodology of Multilinear Evolution.* Urbana, Illinois: University of Illinois Press.

Swartz, M., Turner, V. and Tuden, A. 1966. *Political Anthropology.* Chicago: Aldine.

Tanner, A. 1979. *Bringing Home Animals.* New York: St. Martin's Press.

Townsend, J. 1983. "Firearms Against Native Arms: A Study in Comparative Efficiencies with an Alaskan Example." *Arctic Anthropology* 20(2): 1–33.

Turner, V. 1957. *Schism And Continuity.* Ithaca: Cornell University Press.

_____. 1967. *The Forest Of Symbols.* Ithaca: Cornell University Press.

_____. 1969. *The Ritual Process.* Chicago: Aldine.

_____. 1974. *Dramas, Fields, and Metaphors.* Ithaca: Cornell University Press.

Van Stone, J. 1965. *The Changing Culture of the Snowdrift Chipewyan.* National Museum of Canada, Bulletin 209. Anthropological Series, no. 74. Ottawa: National Museums of Canada.

_____. 1974. *Athapaskan Adaptations.* Arlington Heights, Illinois: AHM Publishing Co.

_____. 1985. *Material Culture of the Davis Inlet and Barren Ground Naskapi: The William Duncan Strong Collection. Fieldiana.* Anthropology n.s. No. 7. Chicago: Field Museum of Natural History.

Von Neumann, J. and Morgenstern, O. 1944. *Theory of Games and Economic Behavior.* Princeton: Princeton University Press.

Wolf, E. 1982. *Europe And the People Without History.* Berkeley, California: University of California Press.

Woodburn, J. 1982. "Egalitarian Societies." *Man.* n.s. 17(3): 431–541.
Yerbury, C. 1980. "The Social Organization of the Subarctic Athapaskan Indians: An Ethnohistorical Reconstruction." Ph.D. diss. Department of sociology and anthropology. Simon Fraser University, Burnaby, B.C.
————. 1986. *The Subarctic Indians and the Fur Trade, 1680–1860.* Vancouver: University of British Columbia Press.